Kaz Cooke attained pub[...] you need to know on th[...] cartoon character called [...] still appears in 'The Eye' magazine. Cartoons and bits of writing have been published in 'The Age', 'The Cane Toad Times', 'The Sunday Herald', 'Dolly', and 'Land Rights News'. She writes a monthly column for 'Dolly' magazine, and a weekly for 'The Age' from whence she pinched most of this book. Kaz has been a journalist and cartoonist since 1981 and in between times has worked for Circus Oz, done silly voices on Darwin radio, been involved in a couple of group exhibitions and developed a strong affection for the spirit of human equality and topiary. She is allergic to cats and engineers.

Kaz's other books include *The Modern Girl's Guide To Everything*, *The Modern Girl's Guide To Safe Sex* and *The Modern Girl's Diary*. She edited *Beyond A Joke*, a collection of cartoons released as an anti-Bicentenary project to benefit the Northern Territory Aboriginal land councils. The book on safe sex was seized by New Zealand Customs Officers after it had been on sale for more than a year, who said they were 'alerted to the likely content of the book by the word sex on the cover'. She was gratified to discover that in the 1960s, New Zealand Customs seized a book called *Games In Bed*, which was a collection of games for sick children.

KEEP YOURSELF NICE

KAZ COOKE

answers your etiquette problems

A Susan Haynes book

Allen & Unwin

Most of this material first appeared in 'The Age'. Thanks to Alan Morison for suggesting an Australian Miss Manners with a twist; Lisa Bennett and Sally Dugan for administering the mailbag, faxing, couriers and filthy mongrel deadlines; and to the readers of and writers to the column. Cindy Donation completed the disgusting task of putting most of the letters onto computer disk. Thanks to encouragers, family and friends including Mum, Dad, Tufty, Ponchita, Pip, Heli, Clarkie, Lulu, D.J. and Redback Graphix. And the most effective agent this side of the French secret service, Janne.

First published in 1990
Second impression 1991

A Susan Haynes book
Allen & Unwin Australia Pty Ltd
8 Napier Street, North Sydney, NSW 2060, Australia

National Library of Australia
Cataloguing-in-publication

Cooke, Kaz, 1962– .
   Keep yourself nice: Kaz Cooke answers your etiquette problems.

   ISBN 0 04 442285 7.

   1. Etiquette—Humour. I. Title.

395.0207

Set in Goudy by Midland Typesetters, Maryborough, Victoria, 3465.
Printed by Australian Print Group, Maryborough, Victoria, 3465.

CONTENTS

INTRODUCTION

The 'Keep Yourself Nice' etiquette column was born in 'The Age' newspaper in Melbourne, in the summer of 1988. The idea soon captured the imagination of readers. They wrote in about everything from what to wear to a semi-formal barbecue to how to prevent newly-retired husbands from trashing the garden.

The column was named after my Nana, who, sadly, is no longer with us, except in spirit. The phrase itself seemed appropriate enough for an etiquette column, although it lacked the unrestrained colour of some of her other favourite sayings, especially, 'You're all over the place like a madwoman's wash-house'.

By the summer of 1990 the weekly mailbag was chock-a-block, running at about 30 letters and by autumn I was wading through about 80 problems, suggestions, complaints, questions and observations every week. Regulars, such as Stultified of Heidelberg and Perplexed of Strathfieldsaye Upper, vied for space with persons claiming to be an order of monks and Wynne, a senior citizen who once threatened a gutter-crawler with a fencing foil in the wee hours..

Recognising the universal nature of its subject matter, all suburbs have been deleted from this volume. Except one. Letters came, and continue to come, from everywhere. Interstate, country areas, the inner city and all manner of suburbs. But the strangest ones come from North Balwyn, a quiet Melbourne suburb often described as 'leafy'. I do not claim to understand this, but it is now a matter of record.

Young people wrote about affairs of the heart and loins, and boys who play too much heavy metal music at school. Slightly older young people wrote about hairs stuck in the soap and being mistaken for 'Yuppies'. Older people wrote about being disapproved of by stuffy offspring, the decline of more lyrical synonyms for bonking, and what to do with prospective daughters-in-law who blow their nose on the table napkins.

Almost all the letters say how much readers enjoy the column, except for those who choose to write three equally dull pages about the size of their willy or berate me for being too trivial. The editors of the Saturday Extra section of 'The Age' saw fit to ignore the willies and give us all more space on the back page. As long as readers and correspondents continue their lively support, we shall be able to keep keeping ourselves nice.

1. TOO ROMANCE

Dates; unrequited lerv; the Great Engineers versus Single Mothers Debate; condom etiquette.

Most etiquette books go straight from the introductions to the section about weddings. This is cheating. Besides, it also displays a rather pathetic grasp of the concept of the forgone conclusion. And misses out most of the really interesting stuff. And anyway, these days not everybody gets married, as even the most cursory glance at the chapter called Rousing Housing will confirm.

Thankfully, there are still some hardy, albeit fundamentally stupid people in whose company I am glad to count myself, slogging away at the general idea of romance, bravely and jauntily thumbing their noses at the cynical assumption that everything will only end in tears, even if their track record is littered with Olympic-standard weeping sessions on a regular basis as a result of lerv gorn wrong.

These noble souls write in with pertinent inquiries on such matters as how to ask somebody to dinner; what to give their girlfriends for an anniversary present and how to cope with a crush. Many letters on such poignant subjects are received, and most are gently discarded, on the grounds that other columnists are well-equipped to take up the slack in the lonely hearts department.

Nevertheless, sometimes a plaintive plea slips through the drift-netting, and thus a great debate may begin. In this way, in advising 'The Girls' about their quest for decent male companionship, a throwaway line about engineering students incurred the whingeing wrath of a couple of engineers, one of whom made a remark about the paucity of available, childless women, which in turn set off a chain reaction of indignant accusations by single mothers. The column's usual policy of having its money on the favourite naturally led it to support the cause of the mums, and hence quite often it still receives letters from cross engineers. This section is a selection of yearnings, deep sighs, cries from

2

the unrequited section of the lovelorn wilderness, and raises the possibility that being 'dropped' is a state of mind.

The etiquette of condoms is an essential branch of modern manners hitherto unexplored, by either Lady Troubridge's stout tome or Debrett's. The obligation to explain things has been taken on board and tackled with gusto, despite complaints from some readers who think it disgusto, many of whom wrote to say they had stopped reading the column but it was still just as disgusto each week.

It is only fair to announce here to readers and the Trade Practices Commission that if I could sort out what every different kind of love really means, invent something to prevent and cure broken hearts and cure all sexually transmitted diseases, I would not be writing this. I would be on my way to accept the Nobel Peace Prize.

Dear Kaz,
What is the protocol for inviting a woman to dinner without any intentions being miscontrued, or infringing on her existing feminist views?

John

THE RIGHT WAY: 'Would you like to come to dinner on Friday night?'
THE WRONG WAY: 'Hey, you with the frock! How about a hamburger before some meaningless sex?'

Dear Kaz,
Is there any proper way of asking a female friend if she would like to start a relationship?

Advice Needed

Whoa boy, settle. You simply cannot bowl up to an unsuspecting lass and ask if she wants a relationship. She may not know. She may want a vanilla milkshake. In which case, buy her one. Start slowly. Ask her out to something specific; if you already know her interests, this will be easier. Mud-wrestling is unlikely. This way, nobody feels crowded and you can have some fun without embarrassing each other. You can badly scare somebody by showering them with rose petals and insisting on a lifetime commitment during the first dinner date. Your friend may be as keen as you are, but a little romance and intrigue, and a lot of humour, are the stuff of relationships. They never went out of fashion.

Dear Kaz,
I would beg your indulgence in the form of advice to help me overcome an exceedingly embarrassing problem. Should one, after the passage of several years, direct one's attentions to someone from all those years ago who, for all one knows, may already be betrothed? Would it be caddish of me to barge back into her life? Does the man from the past always get the girl? If it is permissible, how should one go about such things? Should I write, or telephone, or arrange an 'accidental' meeting?
Nostalgic

Go for it, but there's no call for you to do any barging. Just write a nice note, saying you would like to catch up or perhaps meet for tea and scones somewhere, and take it from there. Do not push the point if your attentions are meeting with a tepid response. And no, men from the past don't always get the girl. Sometimes they get a sexually transmitted disease. Or a broken heart. So go easy.

THE NEXT WEEK:

Dear Kaz,
Nostalgic is looking for me! I am betrothed (oh, silly fool!), have two children and my heart-strings are yearning for tea and scones. How can I make the fairy-tale come true?
Nostalgicess

Look here, this isn't a lonely hearts column. It exists to advise on matters of etiquette and manners, dedicated to the memory of my Nana, who always said 'Keep Yourself Nice'. I'm not sure she would approve of your letter at all. In any case, I advise you to wait for the first approach from the chap, and then wait a while before deciding whether you wish to be betrothed or besotted. Tea and scones is one thing, an emotional upheaval quite another.

4

Dear Kaz,
**What do you do with a man who has pursued you; told you flattering
things about yourself; rung you twice a day, every day; talked of love,
how important families are and commitments between individ-
uals . . . and then dropped you like a hot potato because he doesn't
want to 'get into a relationship'? He's 'unsure'. In other words, the
challenge is over—he wants to move his ego and anatomy to greener
pastures. I would like to kick his emotional cripple's head in, then
spit on him. What is the best way of letting him know what a jerk
he is?**

Aggrieved And Forever Wounded

This is a confused man. Please, under no circumstances, kick him or spit
on him: it will probably prompt him to propose. And as the wedding
cake is being ceremoniously sliced up he will be attempting to have an
affair with half a netball team. Somebody said, 'Living well is the best
revenge', and that is what you must do. It will take time to get over
this, but do not let him know. If you encounter the cad socially, adopt
an absent-minded expression, as if you're almost certain you've met him
somewhere before, which will gently remind him he is of no consequence
to your feelings. Do not let him start the merry-go-round all over again
when he is driven into a frenzy of passion by your indifference. I happen
to know who you are, even though a pseudonym has been used. He will
know what a jerk he is, tomorrow, next week or eventually. That's because
you are gorgeous, witty, charming, honest, straight-forward, loyal and full
of life. He is a fickle and deprived human being. If you retain his photograph,
you may like to practise darts. Try to realise you have been wronged,
but you are not the ultimate loser in this equation.

Dear Kaz,
**I've rung up a girl to ask her out (following your clues on etiquette).
Unfortunately, I spoke to her brother, left a message and I've had
no reply. What do I do? Maybe she doesn't want to speak to me.**
Brad

Brad, Brad, Brad. Let this be a lesson to you. If you want to ask somebody
out, you don't leave them a message. You should speak to her directly.
This goes for girls asking boys out, women asking men out, women asking
boys out and I must say I hope there are no men still asking girls out.

Such an approach is only reasonable. Her brother probably went straight back to watching the cricket and forgot all about the message, or absent-mindedly wrote down 'Vlad rang. Wants to know if you want a trout'. Now honestly, what is she supposed to do with that? Ring again, and make sure you talk to the right person. She will feel a lot more flattered than if she was getting a scribbled message written in non-toxic orange crayon. It would be a nice touch to send her a short note on plain writing-paper, saying you haven't been able to reach her on the telephone and you happen to have two tickets to Whoopi Goldberg, the Melbourne Symphony Orchestra or a private screening of 'Bambi'. Whatever you think will take her fancy. Let's hope it's you.

Dear Kaz,
All of my (male) friends keep getting crushes on me. Is there a polite way to dissuade them?
Sarah

The impolite way to dissuade them, of course, is by saying 'I'd rather kiss a sheep', commonly heard at Young National Party gatherings. The polite way to dissuade is by graciously refusing all attentions, presents and invitations. Perhaps they are after your money. It is unlikely that they are entranced by your modest nature.

Dear Kaz,
My friend wants to go see a band called Brady Bunch Lawn Mower Massacre. I like Mozart.
Cardigan

If some people have put time, effort and, might I add, considerable good sense into coming up with a band name like that, the least you can do is give it a burl. You can take your friend to the opera next week. Lighten up.

Dear Kaz,
I adore my librarian (she is so beautiful) to the extent that in her presence I become slightly incoherent. She has recommended a book to me, and said, 'Tell me what you think of it'. It turned out to be over-full of copulation and other related acts. How do I return it?
Scared To Death

Whack it in the chute and stop reading 'Penthouse' magazine.

Dear Kaz,
The only women who complain are the ones who can't get a man anyway.

Peter

Oh for heaven's sake. Please seek professional psychiatric counselling immediately and stop writing me letters.

Dear Kaz,
What is the appropriate gift for a long-suffering girlfriend on our first anniversary? I've been through all the conventional options such as jewellery, flowers, chocolates, etc.

Andrew

Just how long-suffering is this girlfriend of yours who has been getting jewellery, flowers and chocolates already? Send $15 or $50 to Community Aid Abroad or Freedom from Hunger, and stick your receipt in a nice card saying, 'You make me so happy, I wanted to spread it around'. If she complains, the correct etiquette is to drop her.

Dear Kaz,
Can you help? (I certainly hope so). **I met a man, we felt an attraction for each other.** (Is this person telepathic or did he express an opinon? Was he on drugs at the time and did she check for a wedding ring?) **He was supposed to ring me, but he didn't.** (This does not sound to me like the man was over-endowed with a sense of urgent longing.) **Six months later I was doing my shopping at the supermarket when I heard my name called out above the Muzak. I looked up and realised it was 'Him'.** (Surely you don't mean . . .) **I try to be casual about it, but I nearly fall over. He stands there, stunned.** (Or does he always look like that?) **I saw a small dark-haired female paying for the vegies.** (This is beginning to sound like a police report. Next thing she'll be moving down what I now know to be aisle five, Your Worship, in an easterly direction on the left-hand, right-hand, left-hand side of the carriageway with a shopping trolley, silver in colour, with a faulty front left wheel bearing. Whose vegetables were they? Was the female in school uniform?) **How can I tell if they are together and an item? How can I tell if he still**

likes me? (If he likes you, he would greet you effusively, ring you up, ply you with wit and jonquils. He would not impersonate a packet of frozen mullet in the vegies section.) **Two weeks later I saw 'Him' again and walked the other way. Why do I do this; am I socially inept?** (No, it's because the inner you was being sensible.)

Desperately Foolish

Dear Kaz,
My life has become unduly complicated. As an average male, I could easily cope with a wife in Sydney and a lover in Melbourne. But now, while my lover is out, her flatmate has started offering me breakfast in bed, bringing me fresh towels in the shower and making other overt advances towards me. These are perhaps justified by her thought that 'if he's cheating on one woman, he'll cheat on two'. How do I inform this nice attractive woman that I do not wish to engage in physical intimacies with her?

Worried

Really and truly, is it any wonder I get a bit testy after reading a letter like this? I mean, please. The woman in question does the right thing and politely gives a bloke a cup of tea in the morning and gets him a clean towel. Perhaps it had not occurred to you that she was being nice, rather than hurling herself at you with no thought for her own health. And another thing, Mr Ego, you are going to break somebody's heart. By jingo, I hope it's yours.

Dear Kaz,
I've just started a new relationship and it's getting serious. Who has the obligation to mention, or take responsibility for, contraception?

Besotted

This is a common etiquette problem. Although Lady Troubridge's otherwise indispensable book of etiquette does not mention it, Esquire's book, *The Modern Man's Guide to Good Form*, says quite simply to men: 'Until the two of you jointly and explicitly decide otherwise, it's your responsibility'. I do like this attitude, but would also extend it to women. One cannot assume that one's partner is on the pill, had the snip, or carries a pocketful of condoms. It is extremely impolite to give somebody a sexually transmitted disease, no matter what the occasion, so condoms are now the accepted 'top drawer' form. It is much less embarrassing to have a sensible chat about it than to invite somebody to the clinic later on. In these delicate and dangerous times, be prepared. Others will appreciate your manners in the matter.

Dear Kaz,
We're trying to keep ourselves nice, but honestly, what do 25-year-old, not stunning, not ugly, not fat, not thin women have to do to find a guy these days? Must we be beerily breathed on by guys in pubs? Submit to amateur physical examinations in public (by the aforementioned fellows), or worse still, succumb to Gemini Link, Nexus, Phoenix or some other absurdly named, organised social gathering? To make matters worse, one of us is in an unreciprocated love affair with her best male friend. Help!

The Girls

No. Girls, we do not have to put up with the ill-mannered behaviour of Neanderthal engineering students and the like. We must stride out together to see interesting bands and avoid crushed Top-40 clubs which feature wet T-shirt contests. We must have a good time with our friends in case Mr Right lives in Omsk, and also because if we are sparkling and happy and independent and least expecting it, somebody may offer us a daiquiri and a stroll around Paris. This offer will not be forthcoming if one is lying under a bar stool muttering, 'I can't find a man, and by the way I also seem to have mislaid my dignity'. There are no real answers to your questions except that one's standards should not be lowered under any circumstances. If a relationship with a misogynist nuclear engineer with halitosis is looking good to you, try solitary confinement or a girls' night out. Unfortunately there is a Great Decent Man Shortage. This is not a good enough reason to fraternise with indecent ones. It only encourages them to be indecent, and that simply won't do. Put on your red shoes, sharpen up your repartee and go forth with a spring in your step and a condom in your handbag and leave your simper at home.

On the subject of unrequited lerv, I can only say that it takes two to tango, tickle or tumble, and it's not meant to be if only one is definitely interested. And if you're engaged in a display of self-pity and developing a personal relationship with obsession and crying into your Pimms so hard you can't hear the chap behind you (who looks remarkably like a young Cary Grant) inviting you to Paris, it's your own fault. Good luck.

Dear Kaz,
What's this thing you've got for a young Cary Grant? Everyone looks like a 'Young C.G.' to you. Even Roy Hampson. Why not describe someone as a 'Young Marty Monster'—at least then we know that he's gorgeous, huggable and has reached puberty (deep-voiced). Explain yourself!

Patsy

I beg your pardon, but I am not acquainted, by reputation or otherwise, with either Mr Monster or this Hampson cove. All I know is, when Cary Grant was still supple he was in a wonderful film with Katharine Hepburn and he did some back flips in a scene on a ship. I believe Katharine Hepburn was in possession of a steamer trunk at the time. Now I'm sorry, but that's my definition of glorious romance and I'm sticking to it. I wish I could remember what the movie was.

(*Two readers wrote to say it was 'Holiday'.*)

Dear Kaz,
Your reply to The Girls was disappointing. First, not all engineers are Neanderthal, nor do they universally have bad breath. Second, the Great Decent Man Shortage can be no more than a myth, when not stunning, not ugly, not fat, not thin men like me (engineer, fresh breath, lover of Paris) sit at home alone on Saturday night reading the paper, having given up the search for a decent woman. No decent self-respecting man can be really truly interested in a woman in a wet T-shirt (unless, of course, she were caught in a sudden Paris rainburst). Should you institute the Keep Yourself Nice Introduction Service?

Grazed Knuckles

This, as I keep having to remind readers, is an etiquette column. It is not a dating service, which is precisely the sort of thing that The Girls are trying to avoid. And I don't blame them. Judging by the number of truly fabulous women on their own, or marking time with a Mr Approximate, you must either be very unlucky or not in possession of the full facts about yourself. Either way, I am sorry to hear about it. As I said to The Girls, good luck.

Dear Kaz,
I am reasonably well-dressed and capable of having a serious conversation about all sorts of topics. I do not believe that beer is an aphrodisiac or that I have the right to place my hands anywhere on any woman at any time. I am an engineer and proud of it. So why oh why do you persistently use the drunken loutish stereotype and associate him with 'engineering students'? I have been told that there is a shortage of 'Decent Men'; there is also a shortage of 'Decent Women', so there! I don't feel that either side of the argument can afford to lose any potential 'partner' by the perpetuation of stereotyping. Especially if there are examples around to perpetuate these stereotypes.

Engineer

AND:

Dear Kaz,
I must claim right of reply to explode the myth of 'The Great Decent Man Shortage'. We Decent Men are all out here, but where are these yearning masses of intelligent, single and available, self-supporting, childless women that we hear about? I'm an educated, single, professional man in my 30s, not Porsche-propelled, and I find that, almost without exception, every woman I meet who has anything going for her already has a ring or a lover. Boring! Your comments, s'il vous plait.

Decent

There'll be no exploding around here, Mr Engineer or Merchant Banker or whatever you are. Your letter is as revealing as the one from the other Mr Engineer. What do you mean, childless? Single mothers right out, are they? Not good enough for professional men, hmmm? I'll tell you where the intelligent, single girls are. They're at home, watching Harrison Ford videos or putting the kids to bed, wondering if the pension will cover the gas bill. Perhaps they have not attended university, but they probably haven't had time. Too busy being self-supporting, perhaps, n'est ce pas plume de ma tante croissants methode Champenoise escargot Renault. Engineer: if you read your computer-printed letter closely, you will see that the last sentence is rather revealing. Thank you for your comments. I recommend a good lie down with an interesting book about the history of concrete.

11

THE NEXT WEEK:

By the way, a helpful Engineering Student suggests The Philosophy of Structures, *by Torroja, because it has more history than concrete. Now, a last word on the subject from a single mum:*

Dear Kaz,
I, too, took exception to Decent's comments. At the time I was putting the kids to bed and worrying about the gas bill. Not long ago I was a self-supporting Decent Woman in a demanding job. I am still an attractive, available, intelligent Decent Woman in my thirties and STILL in a demanding job (child-rearing), who is temporarily on a single parent's pension . . . When I mention CHILDREN or PENSION to these 'Decent Men' the shutters go down, the Porsche keys drop out of sight and the hand clutches the wallet and prospects. The 'getting to know you' air disappears and you find yourself propelled in the direction of the nearest bed. THAT is boring.

Decent Human Being

Take that, Decent. Case closed. The search continues.

Dear Kaz,
My hairdresser of 10 years has accused me of being boring and conservative. She has predicted that I will never meet a man or get married and has given me a list of bars and discos I might try to 'get lucky'. She also told me to lose weight, presumably to be more appealing to those men who are going to pick me up. I am feeling offended. Should I take my locks elsewhere? How do I keep myself nice in this situation?

Cutting

Your hairdresser is always right. This is because your hairdresser is holding the scissors and can mohawk you to within an inch of your life if you so much as disagree. Once you are out of the chair, however, you are free to live your own life, get a new hairdresser and eat Tim Tams all day. Your hairdresser was, no doubt, trying to be kind. But your hairdresser does not know your needs and desires, only your ends and follicles. Find another.

Dear Kaz,
What should one do with used condoms? My current bonk likes to tie a knot in them and flick them across the bedroom so they rebound against the wall or ceiling and come to rest in some obscure corner where they are found weeks later. He says he can do whatever he likes with them. How can I persuade him to choose a more subtle method of condom disposal?

Affronted

Perhaps we need a new slogan: 'If it's not on, it's off, and when it's off, it's not on unless it's offed with decorum'. Punchy. I have received several letters about condom disposal. I can only, and first, give thanks that people are not risking infertility, incurable herpes, AIDS or tertiary syphilis. If only everyone would realise that there isn't any more time to bother with whingeing boys and men who don't care enough to practise until they're pretty perfect with a condom. Who needs them? Not us, girls; I'll tell you that for free, just like they do at the Communicable Diseases Centre.

As for this other transgression of accepted modern etiquette, I think you'll find that if you tell your friend that his method of disposal is causing you to have a complete failure of libido, and you are unfortunately unable even to contemplate the idea of bonking, he will come round and behave himself after he arrives. The accepted method of disposal, unless an innovative greenie can advise us otherwise, is to put them in the bin. Don't put them down the toilet. They float in an incriminating manner, or they annoy surfers, or they break down to the ring bit and strangle fish.

While we're on the subject, 'nice' sexual partners can enjoy the office party to the maximum if they have more good sense and condoms than vodka. Make a New Year's resolution to have a full check-up. What do you give the person who has everything? The answer used to be penicillin, but that doesn't work on some things these days.

To Ms Frustratedly Confused: Don't risk your health, fertility or life for a rude boy who won't use a condom. You are not the one who needs counselling. It is good form to discuss the condom question before you get into bed, to avoid this unnecessary scene.

Dear Kaz,
Some years ago, at a point of ecstasy in that most intimate moment, my partner cried out the name of her former lover. How should a truly 'liberated male' respond (just in case it happens again)?
Still Worried

My, that's been preying on your mind! A truly liberated man would probably be able to laugh about it by now. If it happens again, you might try responding, 'OOOOOhhhh, Daphne! Marigold! Trent! Pass the sump oil! Kowabunga! How about a caravan holiday in Marble Bar? The muffler's completely cactus!'. This will draw attention from the mortification of your partner and leave her with the distinct impression that you have a more interesting past than her own.

To Post Neo-Feminist Herbivore: Scottish is as Scottish does and I see nae reason why you shouldn't find happiness, although it is important to find a personality as entertaining as the accent. I like the bit about being able to do the foxtrot and wish you all the best. I used to think that I could be perfectly happy if somebody would read the Yellow Pages to me in a Glaswegian accent. Nowadays I'm a tad more sceptical.

2. NO APPEARANCE, YOUR WORSHIP

BARBEQUE TIARA USES

Clobber in general; women's strides; beards; smart casual; semi-formal; frocks versus gowns; the barbecue tiara.

- **Gloves:** Gloves should be worn when performing home appendectomies; while gardening in heavily spidered areas of the foliage; while driving motor vehicles through blizzards in Canberra; and whenever else one feels like wearing gloves.

- **Hats:** By all means. Baseball caps worn backwards are particularly fetching this year, and large shady effects with foreign legion flaps, peek-a-boo veils and automatic Factor-15 application are most acceptable in areas within cooee of the hole in the ozone layer. Top hats are UNBELIEVABLY stupid, especially at the races. Half a bunch of flowers on the head is very pretty but will not protect the wearer from bees, sunburn, or looking like a twit.

- **Frock:** Dress.

- **Gown:** Long frock. Often worn with jewels or gym boots.

- **Flares:** Aaaarrrrgghhhhhhhh!

- **Red Shoes:** Cheering accessories, suitable for any given occasion.

- **Bow Ties:** More decorative than the usual erstwhile sweatrag. Revolving or battery-operated bow ties will draw attention from another feature best left unnoticed, such as an inability to hold a conversation without referring to property prices. (Likewise with edible earrings.)

- **Medals:** Only to be worn on ceremonial occasions, unless you have one which says, 'Sherriff' (which can be worn on many occasions) and can be used to great effect when teamed with pyjamas, especially after the video shop has closed.

- **Wigs:** The beehive is a good style, and this should be brought to the attention of any barristers and judges who you feel are not making the full use of their headwear options.

- **Evening Wear (Women):** Generally this is an instruction on an invitation to advise guests that they will look a little out of place should they come straight from netball. Usually a frock will do, or an attractive pants suit. Where an attractive pants suit is to be found is anybody's guess. For very formal occasions, a gown of ankle-length is required. This can be teamed with a handy tiara and conversation about the servants. It is, therefore, a great shame that tiaras are in fact at their most useful when employed at barbecues. Spiced sausages may be affixed to the pointy bits of the tiara, which is then re-positioned on the beehive. Practise curtseys before the barbe-cue; the snags will be cooked perfectly in no time. It is best not to pour petrol on the coals during this manoeuvre.

- **Evening Wear (Men):** No shorts, no thongs, no obvious singlet silhouettes and no chundering audibly during the speeches. Formal wear dictates a penguin suit of some description. Various exciting effects with shirt-front furbelows and frills have been made possible with advances in nylon science, but as with many areas of scientific discovery (nuclear weapons, genetic engin-eering and animal species patents) it is best left alone.

- **Safari Suits:** Are you on a safari? Exactly. I thought not.

- **Socks and Sandals:** Upsetting at the best of times.

- **White and Coloured Striped Shirt with White Button-Down Collar:** Stockbroker alert.

- **See-Through Chiffon Blouses:** I know it looks extremely fetching on the twelve-year-old Cleo model, but this is the time to be brutally honest with yourself.

- **Towelling Hats Covered in Bits of Beer Can Crocheted Together:** There is a limit to recycling and it is precisely here.

- **Pink Flannelette Nighties:** These indispensable articles are perfect when one is sick or depressed. When depressed, one should also wear . . .

- **Tatty Chenille Dressing Gown:** Tinned soup stains optional.

- **Jewels:** Send them c/o Allen & Unwin/Haynes, 156 Collins Street, Melbourne, Victoria, 3000, Australia.

- **Fascinators:** A fascinator is a bit of fabric, often in the form of a bow or panel, which serves no real purpose other than wilful decoration. Mostly used as a diversionary device emanating from the waist area, popularised in the 1930s. A modern fascinator can easily and artfully be arranged by tucking a clean tea-towel into one's waistband. Ideal for kitchen teas, as a detachable fascinator of this nature makes a lovely gift.

Dear Kaz,
Could you please advise me about what headwear I should choose this summer, when cycling. Should I wear a floppy hat with a nice pastel colour, contrasting against my tanned body, or should I wear a crash helmet and appear safety-conscious—a positive signal in this AIDS-conscious era?

Pointy Head

Well, well, well. AIDS jokes now, is it? Know any good limericks about massacres, do you? Fond of one-liners on the subject of child abuse? By all means wear a stupid, shallow, floppy, pastel, insipid, pathetic hat to match your tan. If the skin cancer doesn't get you, a semi-trailer might.

Dear Kaz,
I am a 23-year-old woman, and as a relative newcomer to a 'Yuppie' neighbourhood, require some advice as to the appropriate indoor footwear (i.e. slippers) that should be worn. I have been told my well-loved moccasins are best suited to the western suburbs. Should I wear pink fluffy slippers like my Nan?

Country Bumpkin

Anything's better than chillblains. Unless you live in El Salvador, or Canberra. If you're not capable of making an executive decision on your own private footwear, I don't think I can help you. Slurs against the western suburbs have no place in this column. We're all North Balwyn-bashers here.

Dear Kaz,
A local trendsetter was sighted dressed in the manner of a cowhand, dining at a posh pub. At another function, another local identity wore a shirt with no buttons. His wife is very busy, but surely a person of his standing would own more than one shirt. Whatever happened to the trusty safety-pin (two-inch nails are definitely out on formal occasions)? Why has nobody commented on these strange occurrences? Too busy, too lazy, too nice or didn't they notice?

Irish Basket

I sincerely hope able-bodied people sew on their own buttons. If people want to go around looking like Wyatt Earp or Patsy Cline, that's their business. I wouldn't knock back a black suede-fringed jacket myself. Quite possibly, other people are too flabbergasted or intimidated to voice similar outrage at perceived sartorial crimes. Look, it could be worse. Some journalists I know once turned up at a private function wearing Nazi uniforms. They thought it was funny.

Dear Kaz,
I am 71 years of age and live in a retirement village with my husband. Despite being old, your attitudinal column intrigues me. As well as being kind to people and trying to understand them, I keep myself nice by wearing brightish, but matching, clothes dotted with occasional bits of jewellery, not too old-fashioned, although pearls are handy. (Formerly mentioned bits of 'J' mostly donated by various of four sons.) Alas, where I fall down is having to wear flat-heeled lace-up sandals all the time. It is the arthritis, you know. Not to mention really thick tights when it is cold. That is, of course, when I am out of my slacks. The thing is, do you think it is a fair thing, when old, to keep yourself comfortable before niceness?

Young Oldie
P.S. One of the neighbours comes from North Balwyn. Truly. I try to be kind to her, and understanding.

I will tell you a true story. A very young, fashionable and up-to-the-second friend of mine once embarrassed herself in a funky dance club because the hot water bottle hidden under her classy ensemble slid to the floor with a gurgling noise during an energetic moment. I think the moral is that comfort is vital. 'Keep Yourself Nice', as regular readers would know, is a phrase of my dear Nana, who is presently residing in heaven if there is one, finding out that she never has to milk another cow. I suspect she is giving the angels recipes for mince pies and advising the cherubim to wear spencers and woolly socks. If they've any sense at all, they'll take a bit of notice. For variety, get one of the boys to buy you some leopard-skin tights.

Dear Kaz,
It is hard to keep yourself nice when everyone of all sexes is wearing trousers. Do you think women should wear trousers? I don't. It does nothing for them and I cannot see the point in their wearing fly fronts, if you'll pardon the expression. Some have such massive thighs and such vast behinds that it is positively embarrassing. Most say they are nice and warm but continue wearing them in the hottest weather. I value your balanced judgments and would like to have your opinion. They keep running you as a lonely hearts column, don't they? This should shake them up if you use it.

Bewildered

Thank you for your letter. It certainly gave all of us a hearty chuckle. Have you considered satire as a career? You have certainly captured the essential bigotry of our age, especially the more irrelevant and judgmental end of the spectrum. Congratulations: I could put you in touch with a few entrepreneurs, if you're keen.

Dear Kaz,
I am a male person with a closely-trimmed beard. With the advent of George Michael I am constantly mistaken for him in the street. But I've had mine for five years! There are also certain men in blue who assume I'm a thug and I feel I have to prove otherwise. Little do they know I'm a very caring person. Do you think it's sexy?

Soft Inside

No wonder people don't believe these letters are real. Personally, I am not fond of facial hair on men. However, a three-day growth is preferable to a lone moustache. Goatee beards tend to frighten small children and people of discernment. You must decide whether to retain your individuality or a clean police record. Some people find the Don Johnson/George Michael/Derek the Derro/Paul Keating look rather fetching, but it is very rude to subject any really close friend to the abrasive effect of a bristly face. Sandpaper is cheap and you don't have to massage its ego.

Dear Kaz,
I've been invited to a party and I'm not sure whether the person said 'top deck' or 'topless'. What do you think I should wear?
The Volga Boatman

Something about your request suggests yachting. It appears you may have received an invitation from a terse entrepreneur. In which case, nobody else there is likely to spot the difference between topless and top deck, or indeed, between 'investment' and 'paper-shredder'. Wear something with zippered pockets and non-slip soles. Take note of the nearest exits and lifeboats upon arrival. Engage strangers in polite conversation and don't sign anything. Slapping of backs (men) and the offering of outlandish compliments (women) is mandatory at such events. Be polite to the waiter. He probably used to run a merchant bank.

APOLOGY:

'Keep Yourself Nice' last week referred to 'terse entrepreneurs'. This was, of course, meant to read 'Perth entrepreneurs'. While not necessarily wishing to imply that the terms are mutually exclusive, Kaz would like to apologise to any Perth entrepreneurs who feel slighted. We suspect a mistake was made by somebody slurring their words after one too many daiquiris.

OH CRIPES, ANOTHER APOLOGY·

'Keep Yourself Nice' last week explained that any earlier reference to 'terse entrepreneurs' was supposed to read 'Perth entrepreneurs' and apologised to any Perth entrepreneurs who felt slighted. Naturally, the apology was meant to refer to terse entrepreneurs. Discerning readers will have realised that one does not apologise to Perth entrepreneurs, one just quietly steers clear of their banking operations. Kaz is being sent to elocution lessons and the copy takers are getting their Disprin more regularly. Kaz is grateful for the crack team of trained telephonists standing by for your questions on manners. They're waiting for your call. Please speak clearly.

Dear Kaz,
What does semi-formal mean?

Undressed

Semi-formal means the inviting party doesn't want hoons in black tie or bores in thongs. They are having a bet each way, which is how most of us are trying to get through life. I'm afraid I have some bad news: they want you to wear a suit.

Dear Kaz,
Some friends are having a tennis party. What should I wear?

Aquarius

As a person who signs letters with your star sign, I'm surprised you've been invited anywhere at all. You do not say whether you like tennis. If you wish to play tennis, wear tennis clothes. If you don't, turn up in tights, black clothes with ripple-sole desert boots, grasping a lacrosse stick and get drunk, very quickly. You won't be invited on to the court.

Dear Kaz,
What is the correct way to wear a hat?

Veiled
North Balwyn

North Balwyn again. I might have known. Honestly, you people couldn't organise a woodchip in a rainforest. If you don't know that you wear hats on your head, I can't help you. You need someone who charges $150 an hour. No, not the plumber.

Dear Kaz,
What does 'smart casual' mean?

Sartorial

Smart casual on an invitation generally means you'd be well advised to steer very clear of the identified function. You are likely to be surrounded by men in blouson jackets with those shoes held together with bits of string, footwear designed for working on the deck of a yacht. Women are invariably in frocks ending below the knee or in black trousers. If their skirts are above the knee, usually their earrings are very large and possibly gold. Do not wear shorts or anything in rubber. In fact, don't wear rubber under any circumstances, especially if there's a possibility of meeting Englishmen.

Dear Kaz,
I have encounted a problem in making the most of my social life while diligently applying myself to my chosen profession. With time at a premium, I frequently have to hurry from dispensing health to meet my lover. My conservative grey suit, while appropriate in the former situation, is not usually so comfortable in the latter. I have taken to changing clothes in my car as I feel my work colleagues do not need to be encouraged to speculate on my outings. This arrangement is not without hazards, particularly in peak hour traffic and on buses. Have you any thoughts on dealing decorously with this difficulty?
Richard
PS: Why is 'The Age' keeping its postcode secret?

What kind of doctor are you anyway, wearing a grey suit? It's enough to frighten the horses. You're being a bit silly, in my humble, yet solicited opinion. Who cares what your colleagues think? What's wrong with a sense of mystery anyway? I believe you may have what the North Americans call an attitude problem. You do not, repeat, do NOT dispense health—unless a cure for AIDS, diabetes and some forms of cancer was discovered in the past five minutes. Loosen up. You're not God. You can't even work out where to get changed. Actually, it's a shame they've put all that glass around telephone boxes now, or your Superman complex might be right out of control. Do let me know how you get on. 3000.

Dear Kaz,
I am sick of looking like a pig. I have three wardrobes full of op-shop semi-alternative clothes that I no longer feel attractive in. I would like to wear Levis and shirts, but would feel too much like a Yuppie. I have a fairly boring haircut (I'm growing it out) but I do have my nose pierced. Is this enough to retain my individuality? Are tattoos coming back into fashion?

Identity-Struck

Look here, I'm sure you don't look like a pig. Levis and a shirt will not make you look like . . . the 'Y' word, unless you also wear absurdly expensive

23

tennis shoes, compare Collingwood's back line to an opera plot and complain about the mortgage on a holiday home. I am a bit confused about you asking somebody else's opinion about your individuality. Your most individual possessions are your ideals and personality. (And your fingerprints, but perhaps we won't go into that.) Ask Andrew Peacock. If he had a pierced nipple he still wouldn't be Prime Minister. I must warn you that it matters not a whit that tattoos are in or out because they will remain indelible through the non-vogue periods. But you don't mind what's fashionable, do you? You're an individual.

Dear Kaz,
My husband and I have been invited to a black tie dinner for a friend's 21st birthday. Does the tie have to be black, and what should I wear?
Michelle

In short: not necessarily, and probably a frock. Let me explain. Black tie means tuxedo. It means a nice white cotton dress-shirt without silly ruffles, especially if they're edged with powder-blue nylon piping. And a bow tie and cummerbund (that's a big belt thing). Most people will wear a black tie and cummerbund but the brave and noticeable can get away with matching tartan, spots or colours. As long as the tuxedo, socks and shoes are black. If such clothes maketh the man uncomfortable, stick with the penguin look. As for you, my friend, a frock of modest length is the path of least trauma. Personally, I would find it very hard to go past a little black dress.

Dear Kaz,
My problem is implementing a command to clothe myself in 'smart casual' to a country club bash. In my youth I only learnt about formal and semi-formal, so I have laid out my clothes for this evening—a newly purchased tracksuit (casual) and it is really quite smart in a way (warm, baggy and comfortable). However, my up-to-date children tell me this will not do! I will probably be a social failure, therefore, as my children know everything, so give me some advice for next time.
Middle-aged

I am not entirely sure what a country club bash is, although it sounds like a possible Wilson Tuckey fund-raiser. The troublesome 'smart casual' is more about don'ts than dos. That is, don't wear thongs, stubbies, a

24

tuxedo, a ball gown or filthy strides. Especially not all at once. Track-suits, I believe, would fall into the casual category. What you need is a smart, mid-length frock or a decent pair of slacks. Clean and tidy is really all that's required, and frankly I can't see how your children could possibly be 'up-to-date' unless they're living in Paris subsisting on dry biscuits and wearing bits of mosquito net on the front of 'Vogue' magazine.

Dear Kaz,
The barbecue season is well and truly upon us, but I never know what to wear. Sometimes one turns up in a frock to find everyone else in shorts and thongs, and other times one throws any old thing on and one wonders if one ought to have worn a tiara.

Barbie

Wearing a tiara to a barbecue is not a bad idea. One can impale some snags on it, bow down in front of the hotplate for a while and Bob's your proverbial avuncular figure. However, if you do not wish to draw attention to yourself, it is not advisable. Given that one is likely to be dealing with paper plates, tomato sauce, charcoal, kids and dogs, one is acting sensibly if the Givenchy is left in the wardrobe. A presentable frock (just above, or conversely just below, the knee and here I speak of hem-length) is unlikely to frighten the chooks, and a nice pair of long, tailored shorts with a clean T-shirt that does not bear one of the more contentious political messages should suffice. If it is the sort of barbecue where it's contention you seek, may I suggest you purchase one of the garments marketed by the 'Cane Toad Times' in Brisbane. 'I am not American' in Arabic is a good conversation piece, and 'Tony Fitzgerald Fan Club' is a hoot at National Party fund-raising barbecues. No matter what the temptation to wear a wipe-down type of affair, sky-blue shiny leather trousers are most definitely right out. Mind the tongs.

Dear Kaz,
Are moccasins still fashionable as street-wear?

Wondering

Never been overly fond of moccies myself, although I owned a pair of treads once, silly sandals with rubber tyre soles that other children of the early 70s may also recall with shudders. So how could I criticise moccasins? In any case, fashion varies from suburb to suburb, hour to

25

hour, wallet to pocket. If you like them, go ahead. In any case, I think we're squarely in the casual department here, and I wouldn't recommend them for christenings or job interviews. Last time I checked, pink nylon fluffy slippers were poised to make a huge comeback. We can live with that. But let us use this column for a rallying cry: RESIST THE BELL-BOTTOM! We must all stand firm on this issue. I don't need to remind anybody how vital this is. Imagine Mikhail Gorbachev in flares. Cast your mind about the concept of Susan Renouf in satin baggies, Paul Keating reviving V-knee jeans. I rest my case.

To Sensible: I can raise no moral objection to the idea of your wearing a frock to work, but I'm not sure what the other male stockbrokers would think. There's an electrician in Tennant Creek, also a man, who wears frocks most of the time, but it's hotter there. I don't think your employer will be impressed, although you'll probably get into a glossy magazine.

Dear Kaz,
I have convinced my good lady of the advantages of wearing stockings and suspenders in lieu of pantyhose. Should a lady wear her underpants over or under the suspenders? For practical purposes, such as nature's calls, outside seems the obvious choice.
Stultified

Not you again. Last time you were refusing to buy your wife a Whipper-snipper and insisting on giving her another nightie. For heaven's sake, let the woman make some decisions for herself. Now go away. A thought for your wife: Whipper-snippers can play merry hell with hosiery—you may need rend assistance.

3. WEDDINGS, PARTIES, EVERYTHING

THE DANGERS OF A *BLIND DRUNK, BLIND DATE...*

The Particularly Reverend Craig; avoiding vulgarity; smalltalk; blind drunk blind dates.

There are about 748,373,637,489 books and a monthly magazine which can explain in enormous detail the formal, correct and hideously expensive way to plan a wedding. If I might be so bold, I must warn betrothed persons that much of that kind of advice is paid for by the advertising of (and therefore of a nature which will best serve the interests of) the catering, floral and reception-for-hire industries. With jewellers, formal-wear-hire establishments and limousine services getting a guernsey for good measure. They dwell on the commercial, rather than the emotional aspects of a day which is likely to have everybody tired and emotional before the toast, and I speak here of breakfast rather than the reception.

The fewer rules there are, the less likely it is that most of the bride's family will be broke and teary by the time the last can has clattered around the corner. This is not to say that 'Keep Yourself Nice' necessarily advocates single-sex orgies with the clergy or the covering of the best man with honey shortly before the ceremony. But the bride does not have to wear white; a bride for the twenty-third time can wear reams of white if she feels like it, although unbleached is in this year, and a best man can refuse to read out the most filthy telegrams. Betrothed persons would do well to choose a couple of traditions and stick to them. Promising to love and look after each other is a good one—spending $1.6 million on the wedding is perhaps not quite so essential.

There is, however, one absolute rule of marriage ceremonies. Nobody is allowed to get up in the middle of it and shout anything remotely resembling, 'You mad, impetuous fools! Don't do it! Remember the Tweed Heads caravan park, Daphne!'. The time for this sort of talk is before the wedding. If one feels that one is likely to be presented with the unrestrainable urge to do such a thing, one must decline the invitation to the wedding by writing a polite note with no mention of the real reason, and it is not allowed to be on caravan park letterhead, if there is such a thing.

Another area fraught with possibilities of social disaster is the party, and related, vaguely formalised gatherings. Myriad possibilities arise, including uncontrolled flirting frenzies, being the first to arrive, microscopically smalltalk and chatting up a nice lass who turns out to be married to a large man called Squigger who owns a Harley Davidson motorcycle. All these matters can be handled with tact and delicacy when one knows how. It is, however, handy to wear flat-heeled shoes to all social occasions so as to be able to run, if necessary. It is also a good idea to make oneself aware of any back exits leading from the venue, and a handy previous engagement to recall just as a new acquaintance is describing to you the intricate procedure for making tripe.

Dear Kaz,
My partner and I are intending to be married shortly. We have both been divorced. Our burning worry at the moment is, what kind of frock should my partner wear, what colour should it be, and about what length?

Bush Wonderer

The old etiquette books stipulate that re-marrying brides ought to swathe themselves in pastel or cream-coloured frocks. It is my opinion the bride should please herself, within the boundaries of reason. Don't forget: it's your day.

Dear Kaz,
My mother wore black to her wedding 50 years ago to show what she thought of marriage (true). She has surprised everyone again by agreeing to celebrate her Golden Wedding anniversary. What do you think would be an appropriate gift in the circumstances?

Dutiful Daughter

At all costs avoid the golden hamster. Try instead your local nursery for a Golden Moths, a 'terrestrial orchid' with canary yellow flowers. If you know of any outlet for alien orchids, that would be even more exotic. Strenuously avoid the gold-top mushroom, which has hallucinogenic results but could enliven the celebrations no end. Or you could get one of those questionable bakeries to make a big gold-coloured cake with 'humble pie' written on the icing.

Dear Kaz,
What is a suitable wedding present for a young couple who don't have any money. We would like to give money to help out, but wonder if this is a bit vulgar.

Queenie

The best thing to do in this situation is to ask the bride or groom or a well-placed friend or relative of the couple. It may be that a practical and useful gift such as cutlery, sheets or plates is in order. But there is nothing intrinsically vulgar about giving money to someone who needs it. It's much more vulgar not to, if you have some to spare and spend it on historic and gorgeous paintings and lock them in a safe, for instance.

Dear Kaz,
I was taught that to reject a wedding invitation was NEVER done. One always answered, 'We accept/receive with delight and thank you for our inclusion amongst your guests . . . but on that day we will be entering Katmandu on the back of an elephant/attending my grandmother's funeral so reluctantly decline'. Over the years I have found that some read no further than the first paragraph and put us down as another expense or say, 'What's with you? Why accept when you can't come?' Shall I continue as my mummy done tol' me or sink to the depths and buy a 'decline' card.

Manners Maketh Mirth

On no account should you refer to elephants in Katmandu or funerals in a reply to a wedding invitation. The first could cause envy in the bride and nasty scenes at the altar ('You want Tibet?') and the second may depress the betrothed. If you are unable to attend a wedding, write a nice note (not a mass-produced card) saying that you are delighted to hear the news but most disappointed that a previous engagement (so to speak) prevents you from attending. It is customary to send a telegram, but it shall not mention football teams, the bridegroom's penchant for exotic dancing, or the bride's nightie. A simple, celebratory expression of a whacko the chook sort of attitude will do.

Dear Kaz,
I have accepted a proposal of marriage from a dear gentleman whom I met four months ago. I have been divorced for six years, but the dear gentleman has been separated for only nine months. He is being divorced in a few more months, the date of which was filed before we met. This dear fellow has now presented me with a most exquisite ring. Can we be officially engaged yet? Can we openly celebrate our engagement before his divorce? We plan to marry (nicely) at the end of the year. We are keeping ourselves so nice that we're not even living together!

Keeping It Nice

What follows is an opinion, not a rule of etiquette. I feel that it might be a good idea to wait until after the divorce is through, out of respect for the feelings of the dear gentleman's former wife. If you can satisfy yourself that she doesn't give two hoots about it (and perhaps it would not be entirely prudent to accept the dear gentleman's word on this) then I guess you can kick up your heels right about now. I would hazard, however, that if you do not intend living with the dear gentleman before marrying him, that you use the next few months doing a great deal of research on what life might be like with him for every day of the rest of your life. No doubt the last four months have been thoroughly delightful. I hope you can write me a letter in 40 years' time and express precisely the same sentiments. All the best.

Dear Kaz,
My old school friend is getting married. She sent me an invitation, but it's only got my name on it and I wanted to bring my boyfriend. I don't know whether to phone and ask if it's all right, or go by myself.

Capricorn

Look at it this way. Maybe your old school friend's wedding is going to be a fairly subdued sort of arrangement because of the reduced finances of whoever got landed with paying for it. It may be that the budget is planned down to the last sardine, in which case your boyfriend's attendance will throw the entire thing out of whack, leading to one of the great-aunties insisting on forgoing her trifle so that nobody else goes without. Most invitations will say 'and friend' if they wish you to accessorise yourself with a partner. Take earrings instead.

Dear Kaz,
My husband's eldest daughter is getting married. My husband hasn't had a lot to do with the bride-to-be and he's wondering whether he should offer a contribution to the cost of the wedding, or whether a gift will suffice.

Worried Sue

All of the above, if he can afford it, would be a nice gesture. An even better contribution would be an effort to get to know his daughter again, and show her that he cares in other ways besides money.

Dear Kaz,
I have been asked to be a bridesmaid. The couple are to be married under a pyramid in the backyard of somebody called the All-Knowing One for Peace and Enlightenment in Our Times, the Particularly Reverend Craig. The best man is the groom's Kombi van. I have been asked to bring my dog, some incense and a plate of tofu. What should I wear?

Dora

By the sound of this one, you'll have nightmares about facial hair for months. You should wear something comfortable with low-heeled shoes, because you are going on a very long aeroplane trip to the other side of the world that weekend. At least, if you've got any sense, that's what you'll tell the hippie couple.

Dear Kaz,
I am getting divorced. Do I have to give the rings back?

Celebrating

No, but it is correct to offer. The former partner should refuse, and the rings then become family heirlooms or are pawned during the winter if the ex-beloved scarpers with the joint property takings.

Dear Kaz,
I've always been a stickler for punctuality, but these days guests invited to a party for 9 pm don't seem to turn up until after 11 pm. What's going on?

Always First

What's going on is that everyone thinks it's dead cool not to be the first to arrive. The problem with this is that guests arrive in dribs and drabs throughout the evening, look around, think it's a dud party and go on to the next one. There is, however, one thing that hosting parties of the second party can do—have a scheduled attraction. This could be cocktails at eight, an Annette Funicello video starting in the carport at 10.30, or a chance to meet somebody who once had dinner with Susan Renouf at 11. This way you at least give guests something to aim for. Cocktail parties should always be attended at the time specified, ditto for dinner parties and barbecues. Party parties are another matter. If you are first to arrive, NEVER be last to leave. Unless you get asked to stay the night.

Dear Kaz,
When you are talking to someone and they go quiet on purpose and there is no conversation and you are just looking at each other, what do you do?

Brown Eyes

It's hard to know how someone could accidentally go quiet unless they are choking to death, in which case a polite, yet firm, application of the Heimlich manoeuvre won't go astray. I presume a number of your attempts to rejuvenate the chat have failed dismally, and you might as well be talking to a trout. Don't panic: you must escape. If you are at a party, you may exclaim: 'Gad, there's Mervin. I must speak to him about the dog's mange. He knows all about it, excuse me', and hurl yourself into the throng. Your silent partner will not follow you, as mange is unlikely to create interest. If it does, you are in very deep trouble and I suggest you go home and have a good lie down straight away. If there are only two of you, invent a pressing appointment at the stockbroker or Madam Lash's premises, make a polite apology and skedaddle. Here are some handy conversation starters if you are stuck: What Shirley MacLaine will be in her next life (eg 1957 Morris Elite, Yass chiropodist); appropriate

33

punishments for property developers; synchronised swimming. On no account succumb to the temptation to say: 'This is dashed tedious. I think I'll go over there and chat to the trout'.

Dear Kaz,
Is it OK to go to parties by myself? I am 33, I don't drink and drive, I mind my manners, and I'm female.

Party Gal

Of course it's OK to go to parties by yourself. It's absolutely tickety-boo if you leave a party by yourself too, especially if the man with the nylon moustache and droopy shirt near the French onion dip is any indication. Do be careful driving by yourself at night: always lock all doors of your car while on the road and during short stops at the convenience store for extra Cheezels. You might consider always having a mythical other party to get to, so that if you don't know anyone or suddenly feel uncomfortable, you can swan out the door waving regretfully, drive home, curl up in bed and watch a Katharine Hepburn squideo. I really cannot imagine why this question arose. If somebody has suggested that you are in dire need of a companion, may I suggest a blue heeler.

Dear Kaz,
I am planning my 21st birthday party. Are fancy-dress parties still popular and if so, do you have any ideas for a theme?

Uninspired

Fancy-dress parties generally frighten the hell out of people. This should not be so. Guests who cannot afford a shirt can wear a singlet and come as the lead singer of Hunters and Collectors; the pretentious can flounce about in a rented Marie Antoinette frock. Bear in mind that fancy-dress parties seem to inspire writers of murder fiction. To guard against gatecrashers ('You mean you really ARE drug demented cult members? How quaint.') you'll need some tough bouncers. As my colleagues Davo and Bear are otherwise engaged, contact your local right-wing branch of the ALP. Here are some theme suggestions:
• National Party party. Come as a property developer, city council zoning officer or Russ Hinze's knee surgeon.
• Media magnate party. Everyone comes as Rupert Murdoch.

- Reality party. Come as a homeless person, Pan Am security staff or Imelda Marcos.
- Holy-roller party. Come as your favourite TV evangelist or Fred Nile's therapist.
- Queen Mother party. Everyone comes as a short, rich person in ostrich feathers.
- Republican Party party. Everyone forgets the address and no one will admit to sending out the invitations.

Happy birthday.

Dear Kaz,
Having bought a taffeta 'party dress' to wear to a ball, I thought I'd never get a chance to wear it again. However, a wedding invitation to a Toorak address has given me fresh hope. The dress has two net petticoats and a very full skirt. Is it etiquette to wear something that may upstage the bride's rellies, or even worse, the bridesmaids? (I am the groom's cousin.)

All Dressed Up With Nowhere To Go

There is really no excuse for upstaging the bridal party, but that may not necessarily be the case. The bridal party, it must be said, might deck themselves out in waves of chiffon and explosions of tulle. The bridal party might resemble nothing so much as a shocking accident in an unnatural fabric factory. The bridal party might look like nine hot-pink galleons docking at South Wharf during a nuclear ship emergency. The bridal party might constitute a riot of colour, strange rustling noises and bizarre millinery that puts a 1950s Western film in the shade. The bridal party, in short, might be able to get through the entire event without noticing your frock at all. Just to be on the safe side, if I were you, I would consider two main options. First, removing the petticoats for the day so as the frock becomes less phooffy, and second, asking the bride whether she thinks the frock is appropriate. Under no circumstances take the groom's word for it. He probably wouldn't know the difference between a frock and a gown.

Dear Kaz,
What is the correct etiquette to observe when one nightclub bouncer has you in a head lock and throws you on the floor, and his colleague is testing his new boots on one's ribs?

Bounced

I'm afraid that 'I say, you blokes, knock it orf' is likely to be concluded in a strangled cry after the first consonant. There is not much to do at the time, as bouncers are generally bigger than you, have more impressive scars and are usually on rather good terms with the management of the establishment concerned. After the beating, if you are able, try to find some people who witnessed the incident, and you can all drive down to the police station and give statements. (You can have your picture taken.) I am assuming that such an attack on you would be unprovoked. Of course, if you have suggested that the bouncer's mother lusts after Wilson Tuckey, then I think you're on a pretty sticky wicket, morally speaking.

Dear Kaz,
I have to go on a blind date, please answer this letter quickly. I don't know what you are supposed to do. What if I can't stand her? What if she can't stand me? Please advise.
Blinded

First, you do not have to go on a blind date if you don't want to. I'll give you a few pointers on how to make blind dates easier. Each 'datee' should get as much information as possible about the other person. Try to attend some sort of event, screening or performance so you do not have to rely on each other's conversation for about, say, four hours. Do not get really drunk. There's nothing worse than a blind drunk blind date. If, at the end of the date you know you would rather kiss an iguana than see this person again, thank her sincerely for the time you had. Do not, repeat do not, say you will call her if you have no intention of doing so. That is cruel. And unbecoming. Prior arrangements should ensure that you do not turn up in King Gee shorts and thongs to be greeted by a vision in a gown.

4. SUBURBAN NIGHTMARE

TALKING TO THE NEIGHBOURS...

Everybody needs half-way decent neighbours; heavy pets; Mormon dispatch; pointing the toilet paper.

You will have been taught at school about the tyranny of distance, the vast, landed squatters riding picturesque horses for days at a time with only one graduate of the Australian Film and Television School between them, just to get to the next door neighbour's place for a perfectly obvious Trans-Pacific romantic pairing and a hoe-down.

Before the rich and fertile squatters got a hold of the land there were others who travelled on foot for several weeks if they wanted to say 'G'day' to some neighbours, but at about the same time as the rolling and abundant squatters arrived, many of the neighbours were being massacred.

It is about this time that the first Australians realised that they were not to be given too much choice in the way of keeping the neighbourhood in fairly decent nick, and so they fought long and hard as part of the inaugural Neighbourhood Watch Scheme which began in Sydney, performed rather well in Tasmania although it is not in the official records, and was only introduced to the more recently trendy suburbs such as the deserts, North Australia and the wild West in the last 100 years or so.

'Assimilate', suggested the squatters and governments who followed. 'Become civilised and you can have a much better way of life . . . you'll see.' The better way of life is now firmly in place and largely consists of people living in each other's pockets in small boxes called houses and bigger ones called blocks of flats. On a moderate smog alert day, one can see clear to one's neighbour's nostril hair through the side window and can hear a low, cool whistle (the sort Biggles used to make) from the other side of a spit-thin wall.

It is infinitely worse then, when faced with a neighbour who prefers to play classical music suggesting a historical event of great drama and much battalion-type activity at number ten on the volume thingy at approximately 4 am. And of course, there is the dog resembling nothing so much as a medium-sized psychopathic Shetland pony who wanders in next door to deposit several kilograms of excrement, and next door is your place.

Pets, of course, prompted a fair few inquiries about scratching and perving. Dogs were mentioned several times in relation to the aforementioned poohing, but without fencing, it's hard to see a way around it, and duels are no longer common in the western suburbs.

Some suburbs now have dispute-settling tribunals available through the local councils. Although it is not a legal process with the backing of the law, it means that neighbours sign contracts agreeing not to use the dividing fence for firewood, rev the tractor up at 2 am, or put liquid chemical waste through the side sprinklers after dark. Some neighbours will unfortunately not be receptive to this because they are deaf, strange taxidermy collectors who talk to themselves or simply a bunch of complete bastards. Still, it's worth a try.

Oddly, some of the matters which seemed most pressing to column enthusiasts were those dilemmas inside their own house. Some took several minutes from their day to ask whether the toilet paper should roll towards, or away from, the wall. When people worry more about this than what the toilet paper is doing to the environment and whether it will adorn a skiffle board at Bondi this afternoon, well, it's hard to go on sometimes.

Just like the first Australians, many people who live in houses receive unwelcome guests, although nowadays they are less likely to carry guns which accidentally go off a lot, unless you are in a pre-dawn raid area designated by a tactical non-repose group. (T. Aaarrgh. G. for short.)

No, you're a lot more likely to come up against the sales operative, somebody who has been to those seminars where they have to shout about how particularly sprightly (and frankly quite successful, in a rilly parsitive sort of a way) they are feeling.

No sooner have you disabused them of this notion than the doorstep is likely to be almost totally put in the shade by the arrival of the two Mormon evangelists, neither of whom have ever explained satisfactorily to me where all the Mormon women are while the two men are bicycling around the suburbs bearing the message of Someone Fairly Senior In The Bible Department and asking to speak to the head of the household. One friend of mine said they could only stay if they would speak to the dickhead of the household instead. There is a more comprehensive list of doorstop disposal suggestions in this section.

Dear Kaz,
My mother used to say, 'never visit empty-handed'. Does this still hold true?

Dot

Otherwise known as 'knocking on the door with your elbow', this quaint custom is unfortunately dying out. Visitors used to bring home-made preserves or cakes, a cutting for the garden or a lovingly-reared cucumber. These days, visitors are more likely to be bearing an opinion-poll form, the 'Watchtower' or a summons. Indeed, researchers have found that the decline of Western civilisation is in direct correlation to the demise of the 'never visit empty-handed' motto. Makes you think, doesn't it?

Dear Kaz,
My husband and I have a small problem of etiquette that concerns our neighbour. Instead of coming to our front door and knocking, he stands in the driveway and yells out—sometimes my name and sometimes not. This happens on a regular basis. When he wants to speak to my husband in the garden he yells from their side of the fence and conducts a shouted conversation, even though he's on the other side of the fence and can't be seen. I am hoping you could suggest a diplomatic approach. He also yells at his wife, which creates confusion.

Irritated

Next time he comes into the driveway and shouts at you, throw a specially prepared pile of saucepans to the floor with all your might and rush out the front door, colliding with your husband as he hurtles around the corner. This will have to be carefully choreographed to avoid injury. Go into a complete flap and shout back, 'What?!!! What?!! Is there a fire?'. Allow your agitated manner to dissipate slowly and suggest that to avoid panic, he should knock on the door next time. As for the fence business, when he hails you from the other side, say 'Who's that?' suspiciously. Refuse to believe it is your neighbour because you can't see him. 'You may be an alien impersonator! What have you done with him?!!!' you may shout back maniacally. It may be that your neighbour is a person who considers the front door to be a bit out of bounds, except for formal visitors. A mere invitation to use it might do the trick. Other possible remedies include feigning a migraine, enlisting his wife in a conspiracy, and turning the hose on him.

Dear Kaz,
I have two major problems. In our backyard we have a movement-sensitive light designed to scare off burglars scaling the back wall, and barbed wire. Every cat within a 10 kilometre radius congregates to take turns pacing the wall and thus we race to false alarms at least 40,000 times a night. How do we stop our wall from becoming a permanent metropolitan catwalk? My second problem is that my Dad has developed a sudden interest in country and western music. Is there something I can give him?

Amanda

(a) Plant some inpenetrable and thorny creepers and trees on and next to your wall. Remove the burglar system and put one on your windows and doors instead, unless you're concerned about burglars making off with your Hills Hoist or the tool shed.
(b) Patsy Cline, Dwight Yoakam, Tennessee Ernie Ford and Ella Mae Morse.

Dear Kaz,
It's three o'clock in the morning and my neighbour is playing Kate Bush full blast. How do I handle it without causing offence?

Lorelei

Never mind about the fence, burn down their house.

Dear Kaz,
An unsavoury youth (my bridesmaid's son) is causing me stress because
I agreed to board him while he is at (*educational institution*)**. I tolerated**
his wolfing everything in sight, I even forgave him piddling in his
bedroom vanity basin (don't ask me how I knew), but now I find
that he has picked his nose nightly and deposited the debris on the
carpet and the wallpaper. It has set like cement. How do I remove
them?

Iolanthe

Well I'm jiggered. I suspect the lad has been cast in the role of . . . no,
this cannot be explained by undue application to method acting. The
youth must go, and his debris with him. Take photographic evidence and
send it to his mother. One day he will be really famous and girls will
scream at him. Although it is not nice, you can sell the photographic
negative to a newspaper owned by Mr Murdoch and buy some new
wallpaper. By the way, is it too much to ask for some people to send
in some problems that don't make me nauseous? (*See page 92.*) Otherwise
I'm going to throw in the column. This is disgusting.

Dear Kaz,
Our neighbour, with whom we have had good relations for almost
20 years, cut down his swamp gum when the roots were undermining
my foundations. It is now regrowing at a great pace, and he is selling
his property. Should I force him to cut down the regrowth, or, out
of gratitude for his cooperation over the years, wait and make the
new owners do it?

David

I think that out of gratitude you should offer to do it yourself. Hire
a chain saw and pretend you are Arnold Schwarzenegger. Or call a tree
assassin. Your new neighbours might become fond of the swamp gum
stump and force you into years of wrangling through the civil courts.
Don't forget to plant two more new trees somewhere; there's not enough
of that sort of thing going on.

Dear Kaz,
Your constant attack on those of us from North Balwyn reveals only
jealousy. If you've got it flaunt it. Our accountant makes sure we've

got it, and we're thinking of hiring servants. Would it be tacky to dress them in uniforms which match the drawing room sofa pattern?
Upward
North Balwyn

Are you looking for employees or Barbie dolls? I am trying to be wise and tolerant. Please reconsider. There is a lot of unemployment around, and if somebody needs a job badly enough to work for you, then I suggest you treat them with respect and allow them their dignity. Anyway, they've probably got better taste. I hope they pinch your silverware. You'll have some extra time on your hands; why don't you join the Ayatollah Book of the Month Club?

Dear Kaz,
There is a dog living at the house next to my block of flats in (censored) Road. Sometimes I hear it crying and nearly fret myself to death because I don't know if this is serious enough to approach the neighbours politely, and I haven't the guts to storm over and say, 'Give me that dog or I'll call the RSPCA'. Could you suggest a way of speaking to such people or possibly of sneaking into their backyard and taking it? I don't know how to approach people old enough to enjoy that suburban way of life or horrible enough to own a dog and not be nice to it.
Natasha

Some dogs are frightened of storms and will cry whether their owners are nice or not. Some dogs bark a lot when their owners are out. Do not attempt to kidnap the dog, it will probably bite you many times. If you really want to make the dog happier, knock on the door and say something like, 'Hello, I'm from the flats next-door and I'm not allowed to have a dog. I know this might seem strange but I'm a real dog lover. Could I help you out by walking your dog sometimes?'. You may then have to gain the trust of the owners and the dog. Why do you assume that somebody you have never met is practically ecstatic at living in the suburbs, elderly, and cruel? You might find a lovely old couple with scrummy home-made biscuits who love their puppy but are getting too old to walk it every night. On the other hand, you might find a fanatical collector of paramilitary costumes with a well-trained doberman.

'Keep Yourself Nice' has received a swag of letters over the past few weeks from people whose neighbouring dogs pooh all over the garden. This is obviously a serious suburban problem. I would suggest a chat with the dog owners, but that is not a good idea if the owners display psychopathic tendencies, or resemble their Rottweilers. I had heard that containers of water on the lawn do the trick, but I believe this has been scientifically disproved (which doesn't mean to say it has no effect, of course). A friend of mine said that the urine of lions sprinkled liberally about the azaleas is effective, but is not available at most good pet shops. Could readers please contribute to a list of suggestions to combat the problem?

Not a single letter was received on the subject. A good thing too.

Dear Kaz,
How do I stop my boyfriend's cat from sharpening its claws on my legs?
Laddered Stockings

This is a bit tricky. First, ask your boyfriend if he knows a remedy for the problem. If he replies, 'Oh, it does it to everyone, I think it's cute', then you may move on to Plan B in good faith. Plan B is a blood-curdling, sustained scream whenever the moggie so much as lays a paw on your instep. This ought to frighten the whiskers off both cat and boyfriend and, we hope, result in the offending animal (the cat) being put outside. Avoid large floral-print frocks to minimise the possibility of the cat mistaking you for a piece of lounge furniture. Cats provided with a scratching post—a bit of four-by-two with carpet wrapped around it— are less likely to rend the alleged Holeproofs.

Dear Kaz,
I was recently living in a block of flats in Richmond where I had two really nice Greek girls (both sisters) as neighbours. Both are keen and want to remain in contact with me. As I don't believe dating both of them would work, how can I chat up one without offending the other?
Dateless

What an absolutely extraordinary letter. Why is Richmond relevant (I don't mean in the overall scheme of things and the fabric of the universe, just in your letter)? What on earth has Greek got to do with anything in this context? Chat up? I beg your pardon. Two perfectly polite young women wish to stay in touch and you're carrying on like a love-sick puddy calf. For heaven's sake, pull yourself together. Do you have a dictionary? Look up 'friend' and 'platonic'. By the sound of it, any chatting up is likely to offend anybody in the general vicinity. Are they sisters of each other, or somebody else entirely? How would you decide which one to 'chat up'? Have you got some sort of drug problem? Why do people write letters like this? Why am I asking you?

To Besieged: I'm sorry you are finding the attentions of your neighbour unwelcome. If she is expressing views that offend you, or as you describe them, 'racist, fascist and/or chauvinist' on all issues, I can't imagine why you haven't tried shouting. Not indiscriminately, of course, but a short burst of 'I will NOT have that sort of guttersnipe talk in MY house! Be OFF with you!'. As for her wearing lower-cut garments every time you try to offend her, by next July you should be able to call the police, although quite frankly I don't believe you for a moment. The thing is to discourage uninvited visits by saying you are just on your way out, feigning illness or refusing point blank to open the door.

Dear Kaz,
Since my boyfriend recently left me I have moved from the house we shared to a flat in South Yarra. I must say that the neighbours do not seem as friendly as in Collingwood, but perhaps this is my fault. As the new person on the block, should I take responsibility for initiating contact, or should I wait politely for my neighbours to notice me? Also, if the attractive young man in No. 6 leaves his door open, should I say hello on the way past? He is clearly visible on the couch.

New On The Block

Technically it is the neighbours who should approach you, bearing homemade jam or at least some information on the best local milkbar and handy hints on garbage nights. But if they have not made the first move, then it's left to you. You may start a conversation about their garden, the weather, a discreet inquiry as to whether the chap in No. 6 has ever left his room, or a pleasantry about the neighbourhood in general. Don't forget to introduce yourself as a new resident by name, and help yourself memorise theirs by repeating it. Then you can go home and write

45

down 'Myrtle and Phyllis, Number 34' and be able to greet them cheerily. It is good to know your neighbours. Recently some friends of mine called the police when a suspicious-looking chappie entered next-door's precincts. Unfortunately he was the new boyfriend of the daughter of the house and there was mass mortification all round. Still, he could have been a crazed vacuum cleaner salesman, and it's the thought that counts. The police were very nice about it, incidentally.

Dear Kaz,
Which is the most polite direction to point lavatory paper—in or out from the wall? Houseguests point it inwards and it is extremely annoying.
Slushed
North Balwyn

The only time it is important to point the lavatory paper in the right direction is when it is being used for its intended purpose. Otherwise, don't worry about it. The important etiquette about lavatory paper is that your guests are not caught short, in whatever direction.

Dear Kaz,
How do you tactfully get rid of religious persons who go door-to-door spreading their beliefs and who won't go away even after you tell them you're agnostic?
Non-Believer

The behaviour of such persons is beyond belief (so to speak) and if they won't go away, then you can stop being tactful. Without setting the dogs or toddlers on them, some suggestions may help. Try: 'Go away and don't come back'. You see, saying you're agnostic is like a red rag to a bull. They just want to convert you. Allow an alien expression to glaze your eyes, look 'through' them, and try: 'I have already been touched by our Lord, or somebody very high up in any case, and I'm afraid my own faith is so strong there is no need for you here. Bless you'. Another good idea, if you're game, is to proposition them in lewd terms (regardless of gender in any given case). I have found this most effective, particularly with Mormons. Some of them ought to be in the Olympic speed cycling team. Do not employ the same tactics with teenagers trying to sell you something. Say: 'I don't want to buy anything and I know you're probably employed by somebody with a file three metres thick down at Consumer Affairs, so good luck'.

46

THE KEEP YOURSELF NICE GUIDE TO DEALING WITH DOOR-KNOCKERS.

CATEGORY ONE: RELIGION

- **Mormons:** They always travel in pairs and make notes of who asks them in. They shall return. Discuss their undergarments, rumoured to be one-piece neck-to-knee jobs. Why not ask to have a peek? You may then proceed to try to seduce one or both of them. Effective Disposal Time (EDT): 2 minutes. Degree of Difficulty (D of D): 0.0.

- **Jehovah's Witnesses:** Will try to sell you a copy of the 'Watchtower'. Tell them your heavy metal band is about to start rehearsal. EDT: 5 minutes. D of D: 3.2.

- **Evangelical Fundamentalist Christians:** Will speak about the evils of abortion and homosexuality before you even get the door open. Mention that you've never had gay people or pro-choice activists bothering you on a Sunday morning trying to convert you. EDT: 8 minutes. D of D: 5.7. (You may have to leave the chain on.)

- **Salvation Army:** Once a year the Salvos have a Red Shield Appeal. You'd better give them some money if there's any about, because they give it to people who need it. Likewise Red Cross appeals. Always ask for identification. EDT: 2 minutes. D of D: 0.0.

CATEGORY TWO: SALES PEOPLE

- **Encyclopaedias:** Ask the salesperson if you can see the entry on topiary. (The art of clipping hedges into interesting shapes.) It won't be there. Become outraged and ask politely for them to leave. EDT: 10 minutes unless you assault their foot in the door with a handy umbrella. D of D: 10.

47

- **Security Devices:** Quite possibly this person wishes to break and enter at a more convenient time. Possibly not. To be on the safe side, introduce the salesperson to your hound, Richardson, or say that Richardson is arriving home from Attack School tomorrow. EDT: 7 seconds. D of D: 0.5 (with Richardson in attendance), 3.2 (without).

- **Famous Oil Paintings That Will Increase In Value:** They are not and they won't. Express sympathy for the teenaged salesperson who is no doubt on commission. EDT: 5 minutes. D of D: 7.2 if the salesperson cries.

- **Cosmetics:** Do they use animals in the testing of their products? You're allergic. Your Aunty Merle gets yours cheap from the factory. Thank you, but goodbye. EDT: 4 minutes. D of D: 4.6.

- **Girl Guide Biscuits/Bob-a-Job Scouts and Cubs:** Be prepared. Have a small task the tykes can perform. It is wise to forgo the cleaning of the guttering or disposal of toxic waste from the back shed unless you have public liability insurance. Bona fide scouts and cubs can prove themselves by demonstrating a woggle. EDT: 5 hours. D of D: 12.7.

- **Exotic Marital Aids/Tupperware:** Try not to get the two confused. EDT: 2 hours. D of D: 5187.8 if you are trying to arouse your partner with a matching lunch-box and cordial flask set.

CATEGORY THREE: SURVEYS

- **Television Viewing:** You will be asked to fill in a vastly complicated form during the course of a week. Any physics geniuses, electricians, or mothers in the house are best qualified for such matters. It's OK to lie, everybody does. EDT: 15 minutes. D of D: 6.8.

- **Political Polling:** Find out who is doing the polling. Is it a political party? If so, offer their representative a brown paper bag full of cut-up newspaper and wink madly. Watch out for trick questions such as, 'Don't you agree that single mothers are solely to blame for the national debt, the cane toad problem and the strange disappearance of a painting called *Irises*?'. EDT: 20 minutes. D of D: 9.9.

5. HELLO, WHO ARE YOU?

LITTLE KNOWN MASONIC HANDSHAKE

Not being backward in coming forward; introductions; phone etiquette; refusing invitations; lust letters; what was your name again, Mum?

In these modern, confusing, merchant banking-driven days, it seems people have entirely misplaced the manual for introducing themselves, or anybody else. 'Hello, I'm Darwinia, I believe I met you last week at the beer can regatta,' is apparently beyond the reach of most people as a standard effort.

There used to be so many rules about introducing people, it's a wonder everybody didn't stay home except for shopping, and run away if approached in the street. Which is pretty much how many of us behave today, come to think of it.

Remembering that much of our accepted etiquette in the old days came from inbred British dorks with castles full of acceptable currency and a lot of time to waste in between hunting, punting and poncing around on trellised terraces, here are some of the rules which don't apply any more, unless you're practising to marry Prince Edward. In which case I suggest you read another book.

'A gentleman must always be presented to a lady. When an introduction is made between a lady and a gentleman both bow, but they do not usually shake hands. Often it is felt that a mere bow is uncordial and cold, and the hand is held out. It is not strictly correct, except in the lady's own house, and should never be done by a man.' (Ward Locke and Company's *Etiquette for Ladies*.)

This rule has, of course, been abandoned due to stiff lobbying on the part of the Rights For Balding Men Who Wish To Conceal Their Baldy Bits By Wearing Platform Shoes And Incidentally Have No Intention Of Bowing Thank You Very Much Society. Also, after several nasty cases of headbutted titled dowagers, not to mention large numbers of the Scottish royals finding their tiaras impaled on their foreheads after they got home to the Highlands, it was largely abandoned in the real world, although

50

what goes on at a National Party pre-selection meeting nobody knows.

Similarly, the long lists of how to address people that you'll find in other etiquette books are largely useless unless you make it your business to charge about accosting bishops and members of the British aristocracy, and wish to be polite about it. Besides, to address the wife of a baronet as 'Lady Blank' would no doubt elicit a similar expression on her face. And there is not much point in trying on 'Would the Most Honourable Marquis of Dandenong be so good as to desist?', when 'Stop pinching the silverware, Perce, I've got my eye on you' will do just as well.

Many letters to 'Keep Yourself Nice' sought advice on introducing oneself, on public transport, in restaurants, at parties. Many of us are extremely grateful that the 1970s practice of having one's name written on a T-shirt has faded along with flares and scrumpy for breakfast. It was, of course, handy for those whose name slipped their minds shortly before elevenses, but a little tiring for the rest of us.

It should be relatively easy to introduce oneself simply by saying, 'Hello, I'm Mervyn'. Depending on the context of the conversation, it may traverse jauntily in either of several directions with, 'May I sit down?', 'I've got a frock just like that, I'm glad I didn't wear it today', or 'I've been talking to the goldfish for 15 minutes, but I promised myself that I wouldn't leave this party until I had talked with a stranger about the orchid industry'.

The vital thing to keep in mind when one introduces oneself is that one may be disturbing the other person. The other person may think one reminds her of nothing so much as a dead ringer for a perspiring and persistent man who once accosted her in a darkened disco and tried to sell her shares in a polyester shirt factory and then tried to look down the front of her dress, losing his glass eye in the process, which rather smartly came to rest in her Pernod.

The other person may be a very shy chap who has just come from home where he found that his girlfriend had departed in company with his cheque book, the occasional furniture, the dog and his unique plan for revolutionising the tea-bag, not yet patented. He may not wish to chat with somebody he earlier overheard in the kitchen saying, 'Men! Honestly!'.

One must be prepared for the rebuff, and one must accept it with good humour.

Thus, if a person responds to a polite self-introduction with 'Big DEAL, anyway,' or 'Get RIGHT away from me', it is polite to retreat. If however, the object of one's attentions attempts to throw one from a moving train, pour sherry over one's head or shouts, 'Repent, repent, for the Valley of the Shickered Vikings shall rise again and smite thee on the boko with the force of 10,000 whangees shortly', it is perfectly acceptable to take low-key evasive action.

For those interested in clearing up the problem of handshaking or not handshaking, when in doubt, offer your hand. It is unlikely to be rejected. The shaking of hands, except in more radical chapters of the Masonic Lodge movement, is supposed to be a dignified affair. It has nought to do with impersonating arm wrestling, pulverising ligaments or teaching a pensioner with arthritis the effect of a good, hard grip previously employed only figuratively by the banks. Nor is a handshake to evoke memories of attempting to catch a dandelion seed, grasp a small flathead or tickle a sponge-finger. Women shake hands too, if they wish.

One should never kiss another person unless one is prepared to bet more than $75 that the other person will like it.

And it is here we solve the age-old dilemma of walking down the street with friend A when one bumps into acquaintance B. At this moment, one will have forgotten A's name entirely, and possibly B's, and be fairly unsure of one's own, come to think of it, making introductions a tad on the awkward side. Read on.

Dear Kaz,
This really embarrassing thing keeps happening to me. When I'm out
and about with a friend, I often meet an acquaintance. The problem
is that I completely forget the name of the acquaintance and chatter
on without introducing them because I don't want to reveal my
forgetfulness. Which is more rude, not introducing people or saying
'I've forgotten your name'?

Friend Indeed

There are few more embarrassing social situations, apart from the ones
involving green peas, fish knives and bishops. But it does happen to almost
everyone. The accepted method is to clutch the forehead (not unlike
Sarah Bernhardt), allow a wild expression to play about your eyes and
say: 'Golly, I've been so frantic this week and now your name has gone
totally out of my head. Honestly, I'd forget my own mother'. To which
the acquaintance will reply: 'I am your mother, stupid'. Or 'I've forgotten
yours, too, I'm Mervyn Purvis from macrame class'. You should then commit
the name to memory by repeating it while looking into the person's face.
'Mervyn Purvis, of course! Mervyn, I'd like you to meet . . . oh hell, it's
on the tip of my tongue.' If you don't establish somebody's name, the
situation will get worse at every encounter. Better to be thought a
scatterbrain than a snob.

Dear Kaz,
I travel to work by train, and would like to say something to a young
woman who gets the same one every day. How should I start?

Grigor

According to Lady Troubridge (a standard etiquette reference for more
than 50 years), a gentleman on a train may help a lady with a window,
'but it is incorrect for him to attempt to open a conversation with her
or to intrude upon her in such a way on the strength of his service'.
It does not say what to do if the lady is intent on smashing the window
so she can slash the upholstery with broken glass and the gentleman is
writing 'IRON MAIDEN ROOLS' on the door. Perhaps you might start
with a smile, and a polite comment about the book she is reading, the
graffiti on the last station or your opinion of the American Vice-President.
Do not feel too hurt if your efforts are rebuffed. Quite possibly the last
person who spoke to her on a train said, 'Give us your purse or we'll

kill you'. And she may be a little distrustful of a Northern line, however original.

Dear Kaz,
I had a good friend in high school but I don't know if she would regard me as a friend any more. I moved to Sydney and lost touch. When she came to Sydney for a while to work, we caught up again but to the detriment of our friendship I was into band management, I was sexist and manipulative. She commented that I had changed and we went our different ways. That was five years ago. I believe I have grown up since then (whether it's biology or social conditioning, boys take longer, and some of us never grow up) and seeing your column in 'The Age' I decided it was time to patch up a friendship. How do I indicate to you that I'm a good and proper person? Do I send references? Do I tell you I've been in a steady relationship with the most wonderful girl in the world with the inference that I must be OK to have such a wonderful person like me? Or do I simply say write to me, I'd really like to hear from you. Your mate,
Tim

Welcome back to the real world, old son! I believe your letter has struck exactly the right notes of flattery and apology, and is an example to all of us who have behaved like weasels at some time or other. A postcard is on its way. (By the way, if you still behave like a weasel, I shall have no compunction in revealing the Science Block Incident to the most wonderful girl in the world.)

Dear Kaz,
A couple of weeks ago I remembered a boy I knew in Grade Three, before I left that school. I met him again briefly six years ago. I have found out where he lives and I want to get in touch with him. How should I go about it?
Hip

If you know where he lives, I suggest you also find out his sexual preferences, marital status and employment details. If you can find out where he works, you may contrive a 'chance' meeting, and suggest a drink at the local to catch up on each other's news. (That should take you a while, perhaps you could skip Grade Four and Form Three.) I would not suggest vaulting his front fence and feigning unconciousness on the lawn. He is likely to get suspicious. If all you have is an address, write him a short note saying a mutual friend gave it to you, and you'd like to meet him to chat about old times. But don't push it if he says 'no', or 'I just have to put the babies down, wait for the sitter and go and pick up Angelique from work'.

Dear Kaz,
How do I introduce my misogynistic old school friends to my radical feminist university friends without inciting a riot and without jeopardising my ideological integrity?

Rowan

Why would you want to do that? You're just looking for a fight, aren't you. Dull this week, is it? If you happen to meet a misogynist while out with a feminist (or vice versa), it is correct to warn each party during the introduction. 'Clair, this is Baz. Bazza writes the captions for "Penthouse". Baz, meet Clair. She runs a refuge for battered women in the western suburbs.' Then run like hell. If forewarned of the meeting, have your money on Clair.

Dear Kaz,
I'm a part-time artist and a part-time nurse. The deputy matron where I work has more developed sensibilities than the matron. Should I invite only the deputy to my next exhibition opening?

Anxious Aesthete

If you paint in five-centimetre-thick black and red oils, mainly depicting the eternal dichotomal angst of naked, bald drug fiends in chains, then it is only fair to warn the matron. But I think you should invite her anyway. If you can afford it, the invitations could carry a reproduction of your most offensive work. This would allow a gracious refusal on the grounds of a previous arrangement. (Do check with the deputy about the matron's coronary history first.) Look on the bright side—she might buy one for the psych ward.

PS: Why did you choose the two most ill-paid jobs in the universe?

Dear Kaz,
My little brother answers the telephone by saying: 'What do you want?'.
Another thing I hate is people who ring up and say, 'Who's that?'
before you know who they are. What is the correct telephone etiquette?
Engaged

Callers should always announce themselves without undue fanfare. 'Hi,
this is the incredibly zany Trent, looking for the adorable Mindy,' is replaced
easily with 'Hullo, it's Trent. Is Mindy at home?'. This also allows Mindy
to bribe her brother to say: 'Mindy has gone to Zimbabwe. She may be
gone for quite some time. She said to tell you to have a nice life'. If
you answer a friend's telephone, ask the name of the caller. Your friend
will assess the situation vis-à-vis the difference between Acme Debt
Collectors and Steven Spielberg's casting agent. It's called 'screening'. Don't
have an inane message on your answering machine. You want people
to know that you are out, not that you are a complete bimbo. When
answering your own telephone, say whatever you like. You pay the bill,
and if you want to pretend you're the Queen of the Nile, it's your business.
Especially if you are expecting a call from Trent.

Dear Kaz,
When refusing invitations is it polite to give a reason? (Previous
engagement, travel abroad, etc). What should one do if one is just
disinclined to participate in a particular event? Be a charming liar
or a boorish speaker of the truth?
Not Going

You can say you have to be at the Ferret Fanciers Meeting until the
cows come home, but one day you are probably going to get a non-specific
invitation. Something, perhaps, along the lines of 'Would you care to
come scuba diving some time? I have a small island near Samoa'. If you
keep telling lies to somebody, they will persist. For example, if you are
invited to participate in a strip and prawn evening, you should not feel
obliged to pretend it's your night to put out the garbage and floss the
dog's teeth. You may say firmly, 'I think I'd rather die, thanks all the
same'. The trick is to aim for being a charming speaker of the truth
and, when occasion demands it, being a boorish liar. I hope you're not
a politician or you'll get it all mixed up.

Dear Kaz,
Having recently decided my couch was due for a facelift, I contacted
an upholsterer. He turned out to be a 65-year-old with a penchant
for frequent visits. While explaining the relative merits of jacquards
and velvets over yet another cuppa and the last of my Scotch Fingers,
he asked me out to dinner. Not wanting to encourage him, I politely
declined. Unfortunately the invitations are continuing thick and fast.
HELP! Is he a lonely old man or a sleazebag? I'm 25. PS: Purple velvet
or lime-green vinyl?

Undecided

You should tell the man that your relationship is a business one, and
you would feel more comfortable if he stopped asking you out. There
is no evidence that he is a sleazebag, quite possibly he is very interesting
and would make an entertaining friend. That is up to you. You sound
like a kind person, if a wary one, and I know you will be polite. I cannot
comment on matters of personal taste in interior decorating, but will
venture to advise you that with summer coming on, any kind of vinyl
is likely to get you into another sticky situation.

Dear Kaz,
I have been captivated by the wit and prose of a newspaper feature
writer whom I have never seen. Would it be proper for me to propose
a meeting to her? If so, how?

Captive

Enjoy the wit and prose. Do not risk discovering that your idol favours
neat vodka before breakfast and fondles waiters. Compose a charming
fan letter if you must, but cherish admiration from afar. Should you contrive
a meeting through other means, well and good. But journalists often receive
strange letters, many written in coloured pencil on brown paper bags
about alien landings in North Balwyn. Your proposal is probably destined
for the Alien file, I'm afraid.

TWO WEEKS LATER:

To Captive: Thank you, but I am presently satisfactorily romantically
involved with a boy and a blue heeler. I live in Darwin and cut my toe-
nails with a rusty Stanley knife.

Dear Kaz,

As a result of an accident a few years ago, I am now a wheelchair user. I'm not that old really, I still look pretty good, and I'm quite a friendly person. Many of my friends greet me with a kiss these days, probably more than did in the past, and since I can't shake hands too well, I guess that is understandable. However, some people whom I feel I don't know well, such as elderly gentlemen friends of my parents, or neighbours, also adopt this form of greeting. On such informal occasions I would prefer a simple, verbal greeting. I've tried saying: 'Good morning, Mr Codger, how are you, please have a seat,' with some success at the hello, but I still get the goodbye kiss. Is there a nice way to restore and create reserve?

Kissed

If your wheelchair is motorised, I suggest you do a wheelie and keep moving away from insistent kissers at a cracking pace. Possibly you could zoom around them in circles until they get dizzy and give up, although you might get dizzy too, which won't do. The only thing I can think of is to say loudly and sharply, 'No! don't kiss me!'. When asked why not, there are several possible responses. 'I prefer to shake hands/just say goodbye'; 'Who do you think I am, Sleeping Beauty?'; 'Because I'll run over your foot'; 'I only kiss members of my immediate family'; and 'The last person to kiss me developed Fortesque Skin Crawl and I'd rather you didn't risk it'. Further suggestions from readers may be forthcoming, and I shall pass on any worthy ones.

Dear Kaz,

Re: kissing. A single garlic clove held in the mouth is all that's needed. As the would-be smoochers stoop down, crunch it between the teeth and exhale sharply in the direction of the smoocher. The result should render the assailant momentarily insensible, allowing enough time for evasion.

Martin

BUT what if the kissee wants to be kissed by somebody else, or they can't bear garlic themselves? It's a tricky one.

6. EAT, DRINK AND BE WARY

Diverting ways with fish knives; dinner flirtations; in the soup; drunks; eschewing chewing.

There are not so many table manners rules any more. The one about using a special escort to bring in the tucker while everyone takes their hat off before bowing and kissing the other diners has inexplicably gone the way of the drop-kick. Other rules still remain law in most homes: do not hurl the spinach at your sister in such a manner; do not say 'Kerist! What's this stupid soup thingy doing on the table, Trixie?' when a finger bowl appears between courses; and always offer your mate the last dim sim.

Luckily, we have a fairly informal style of partaking of the sustenance of life, and thus, it should not matter too much if you put your bread roll in a sherry glass by mistake. Dinners at which one is confronted with 47 forks and a full range of early Celtic weaponry on the right-hand side of the plate should be less of a traumatic ordeal if one knows to start from the outside and work one's way in towards the crockery, course by course, unless one is allergic to the fish, or one is given marinated squid-inked lark testicles au gratin before 7 pm or passes out accidentally into the boiled ice-cream on a coulis of feral radish botties. Got that?

Napkins, of course, can be paper ones in which case somebody is going to be involved in an ugly argument about the timber industry before pudding, or of heavy linen stuff which is harder to blow one's nose on in an emergency situation after the horseradish soup. Napkins, also known as 'serviettes' and always called 'serve-you-rights' by a particularly witty male relative at every single sodding Christmas dinner since you can remember, may be folded into enticing origami designs, most notably a swan, a bishop's hat and the Charge of the Light Brigade (from a rear advantage).

Food is always served to each person from the left and removed from the right, unless somebody has to be given a substantial bribe to clear the table. It is customary to wait until the person has laid waste the food on the plate before removing it, unless the person has expressed the considered opinion that if they see broiled cabbage one more time this week, regardless of how the pension is holding up, they will be forced to adopt regurgitative action on a unilateral basis.

Eating sins include mastication with one's mouth open unless one has sinus blockages; unannounced food fights when one side of the table has just dispensed with their blancmange and the opposing forces are well-equipped with banana purée and a phalanx column of lime jelly; tripe; conversation about animal husbandry; the preferential voting system, and any mention of what flies are before they grow up.

Diners may feel free to set about a companion who is smoking cigars at the table. Cudgels may be provided for this purpose.

That's enough now. I believe readers with common sense will have a pretty fair grasp of things. Other items on the agenda include when the ladies should leave the dining room; the precise uses of a fish knife; dealing with frenzied flirting at the table; sharing restaurant tables with strangers; tea-bag etiquette and what to do when you bring a bottle of wine and your hosts hide it and serve something resembling nothing so much as sump oil vinegar.

And remember the vital rule of drinking: should a friend or colleague attempt to operate a motor vehicle while under even the slightest influence of alcohol, it is correct etiquette to wrestle them to the floor, hurl their car keys into the nearest major irrigation scheme feeder, tie them to the shed door or otherwise use necessary force to stop them going out and murdering themselves or somebody else. This technique is much favoured by experienced hostesses who know that thank-you letters received from the local lock-up or burns ward lack that certain charm one has come to expect, and the stationery is usually pretty substandard, come to think of it.

Dear Kaz,
I have the most disturbing problem. A possible prospective daughter-in-law has the most distressing habit of blowing her nose on her paper serviette while sitting at the meal table and then returning it to the table, sometimes to have another blow. You may well ask why don't I use double damask table napkins but that may only encourage her. Kaz, I implore you, what do I do?

Distressed Matriarch

Firstly, be grateful that your young friend does not use the tablecloth. Secondly, if you are dining at her home or a restaurant, carry some spare hankies in your handbag and offer them to her as she blows her nose, saying, 'Oh here's my spare hanky, Daphne, please don't waste your serviette'. At your home you may say, 'Oh, Daphne, what must you think of me, here's a hanky, I'll get you another serviette'. Also, give the paper serviettes a miss wherever possible. They use up trees and encourage nose blowing. Try not to be too downhearted if Daphne marries your pride and joy. If this is her worst habit you're not doing too badly. Remember the old joke, 'About the best thing I can say about my son's girlfriend is that all her tattoos are spelled correctly'.

Dear Kaz,
Should ladies still leave the dining room before the gentlemen?

Cigars And Port
North Balwyn

If the alleged gentlemen really are from North Balwyn, I suggest the alleged ladies should vacate the room by the nearest available exit at the earliest opportunity. You people are completely bonkers. What do you think this is, upper-class London in the 1890s? There is something seriously wrong with your suburb, and this sort of letter MUST STOP!

Dear Kaz,
When should I use the fish knives?

Bemused

This is an easy one. The fish knife is used when stabbing a wandering hand under the dinner table, when unscrewing a piece of electronic equipment in the dark and for cleaning one's fingernails when nobody is looking. And for eating fish.

Dear Kaz,
I simply cannot bear eating noises produced by people who chomp with their mouths open. How do I tell them to shut up, without being thought of as neurotic?

Jane

You can't, because that would be even ruder. It may be you have struck somebody who cannot breathe through their nose and therefore will keel over if forced to eat with their mouth closed. Try to be selective in your choice of masticating partners. Try not to worry about it too much, worse things happen after CIA meetings.

Dear Kaz,
An ex-colleague from Sydney, recently separated from her boyfriend, came to Melbourne on a business trip. I've only been down here a few months, and, with all of my friends and family in Sydney, was looking forward to her visit, so I organised a dinner with a few people, including my beloved. But alas, she spent most of the night flirting with my beloved, and though he did not reciprocate her attentions, I feel miffed because she barely spoke to me. Should I have said something to her? I feel a little betrayed and neglected.

Confused

It's difficult to say something useful at the time. 'Excuse me Clarice, could I interest you in dessert? I'm afraid you'll have to put Clive down if you wish to eat it with a spoon' may be considered a touch pointed. 'Clarice, if you don't stop fondling Clive's ankles and speak to me, I shall probably cry' is a little pathetic. Still, perhaps your friend was temporarily demented, in which case it would be a shame to trash the friendship without further clarification. Perhaps you could tell her on the telephone or in a letter that you felt neglected by her. If she says she's terribly sorry but her mind has been unhinged by lost love in Sydney generally, you may resume normal services. If, however, she asks for your boyfriend's telephone number, you may cross her off the party list forthwith.

63

Dear Kaz,
I simply love cooking, but I have come up with a problem. When
I am cooking escargots in garlic and butter sauce, how do I get the
escargots back into the shells to serve them to my guests? Please keep
up the good work with your absolutely darling little column.

Maggie
North Balwyn

Whacko the diddle-o, another letter from North Balwyn, although mys-
teriously postmarked in Blackburn. Thank you so much for your kind
thoughts; it's a bit like being praised for a good human rights record
by General Pinochet. If you must eat snails as a way to cut costs, and
keep up appearances, I suppose you must. Although I hear that aphids
in aspic are big in North Bawls these days. Your specific problem will
be easily overcome by the deft use of a crowbar and a chic culinary aid
known to French chefs as Tarzan's Grip. A little dab'll do yer.

Dear Kaz,
I have just moved to Canberra with my job. Everyone here drinks
a fair bit of alcohol. Any excuse will do. My problem is that I end
up driving all the drunks home because I'm usually sober. (Yes, I do
work for the Public Service.) Should I drink more, or drive more?

Ms Anthrope

Neither. Get yourself some new friends, and make sure they are not
journalists.

Dear Kaz,
I took a bottle of Grange Hermitage to a friend's dinner party last
week. They put it in the cellar and served Chateau El Cheapo all
evening. How can I ensure this doesn't happen again?

Thirsty

For a start, you ought to know better than to go to dinner with people
who have something called a cellar. That's asking for trouble. But if you
really want to make a point, without being as rude as your friends, you
might, in a studiously casual tone, ponder the merits of a particular Grange
Hermitage, because you're not sure whether to buy that vintage again.

But don't expect to be asked back for a free feed. On no account should you say loudly upon leaving: 'Well, I'm orf. Where's me plonk?'.

Here's a question and answer from Bill. This is the only time I will encourage him because he made it all up and besides, it's pretty funny.

Dear Kaz (he means Bill),
I am embarrassed whenever I see my old high school teacher in a pub. What should I do?

Johnno (he means Bill)

Social etiquette requires that you approach the teacher and say, 'Sir, I bet you never guessed I would end up like this'. The teacher is obliged to reply, 'Well, if it is not Goulopoulos of 4B'. It is not your place to tell the teacher that you are not Goulopoulos and you were never in 4B. You are merely required to say, 'What are you drinking, sir?' and buy him a beer. This is why the teacher is hanging around hotels in the first place.

Dear Kaz,
I am college-educated, articulate and confident—but totally insecure when it comes to tea-bags. Having fallen on hard times I buy the stringless specials and in the privacy of my own home, nearly choke on the beggars. Now listen, when my more affluent friends arrive, do I have at the ready the designer labels that dangle out (and where do I suggest they put them after use?) or do I keep on with the stringless beasts, this time in a teapot? It was never this hard when we were all into wine, at least then I knew how to follow the instructions on the box. Please help.

Bag Lady

First, stop pandering to your 'more affluent' friends. If they're that keen on decent tea they should bring you tins of Earl Grey, as well as the new novels they have read and cuttings from their garden. As to the disposal of tea-bags, they should be delicately removed from the cup with a spoon and flicked deftly across the room into the rubbish bin. A score card may be kept on the fridge with two points for each successful fling and three points for a classy rebound. The winner at the end of the tea break can have the last Tim Tam. Look, I'm sorry, I find it very difficult to deal with this. It's a sunny day and I'm chained to the typewriter soothing a tea-bag case.

Dear Kaz,
A friend and I decided to dine out in a busy little Italian restaurant in a well-known suburb of Melbourne. The only way we could get a table was to share with a gentleman who was dining alone. We said 'hello' as we sat down, but then I was unsure as to whether I should engage this gentleman in social intercourse over our lasagne, or whether I should let him dine in peace and quiet while I chatted with my friend. I didn't want to appear rude and ignore him, but at the same time I didn't want to impose and disturb what may have been a quiet, relaxing dinner for one. Your advice on this matter would be greatly appreciated.

Socially Inept
North Balwyn

I am astonished to receive such a sensitive letter from North Balwyn. Thank you. When 'forced' to share a table in a busy restaurant, one is not required to make conversation. However, if you feel chatty, and your attentions seem welcome, there is no reason why you can't have an interesting conversation. You might test the waters, after a fashion, by making a witty plea for inside information on the standard of fare. But heed this warning: when sharing a table, do not indulge in gossip. It's odds on the unknown person is the second cousin of the boyfriend's uncle's boss whom you are picking to bits over the entrée. You may think this unlikely. It isn't.

7. ROUSING HOUSING

Married or living together; shared houses; the great hair-shedding controversy; a loose spouse aroond the hoose; International Short, Fat, Grumpy Men's Day.

Very few people who have made our acquaintance have exactly the same opinions on how to hang out the hosiery; who took the garbage out last time; whether tea leaves can be dumped in the sink or the umbrella stand in the hall; whether it's all right to bring psychoanalysts home for tea without warning; if squid should be boiled into lard on a slow heat for most of October; which side of the bed is best; how many weeks you can leave a sink full of dirty dishes; which cleaning fluids are most likely to emulate Chernobyl on an environmental impact scale of things; and whether that particular shade of acid green is completely right for the lounge room walls.

Thus, this portion of the book is devoted to promoting domestic harmony, making it easier for people to live together, or perhaps just trying to keep raw violence at bay. Whether house-sharers are related by extended family, marriage, a shared interest in the early works of Ken Done, or because they answered an advertisement in purple felt-tip stuck to the window of the milk bar with bubble-gum, problems crop up regularly. Sometimes, flatmate relationships are made in heaven. One person is slovenly and the other ovenly, and that's the way they like it. But there are tenants, or housemates, who ought to be provided with a surrogate old-fashioned mother (as depicted in margarine advertisements), if they are going to have a decent crack at getting through life without other people shouting at them a lot.

You, however, are not this person's mother. So if he or she has not done the dishes in several months, his room is beginning to send olfactory signals reminiscent of the Werribee tip through the rest of the house, and she didn't seem to realise that toilets were not self-cleaning, then this person will have to be asked to leave. Unless, of course, you are married to this person, or planning to spend your next few summers together on a regular basis, in which case there will have to be some hefty re-training scheduled.

Falling in love does not necessarily mean that you will agree on the allocation of chores as well as soppy movies and abseiling for fun. Being under the same roof entitles one to be able to make observations of a personal nature that would be unsuitable in other situations. The biggest single controversy of shared housing in our times, it seems, is hair left imbedded in the soap. It may not seem like a major life issue to me, but after seven letters over a few weeks complaining of the same matter from far-flung, fraught households, it seemed a good idea to give the subject a run.

Dear Kaz,
My girlfriend and I are intending to live together soon, rather than take the traditional path of getting married. As a point of modern etiquette, should the male seek permission and the blessing from the defacto in-laws, or should it be treated as just a further step from being lovers?

Living In The 80s

Ask your girlfriend. In our family, we prefer the term 'out-laws'.

Dear Kaz,
We have a problem. It's a problem of etiquette, just your field. While visiting a close friend and her new lover (who is also a close friend and an ex-lover), who are both very NICE . . . please tell me when is the right time to leave and let them bonk each other senseless? Should it be when you have established that the film you were going to see isn't on; is it when you return from the bathroom and they are kissing; should it be when they start cutting each other's fingernails, or when?

Ms Raspberry

69

Yes, by the sound of it. They may not be bonking at all, only gazing pathetically at each other. It is a matter of international amazement that people who are in love can together be interested in dog clippings, the collected thoughts of engineers, or watching grass grow. I think frenzied kissing is probably a good cue to skedaddle, but why don't you establish a friendship in which you can ask, 'Shall I go?', and they will say, 'Yes, by all means, we wish to engage in some serious spooning', or 'No, no, don't mind us, we're just a trifle smitten'. Or work out a secret signal with your girlfriend. When it's time for you to leave she can whistle the National Song of Scottish Unity (I'm sure there is one) or put on a pink hat with especially coquettish trimming, or wave a tea-towel in a recognisable semaphoric or soporific pattern.

Dear Kaz,
As is my wont, I had planned to present my dear wife of 26 summers with a pretty nightdress to mark the occasion of Christmas. Now, without inquiry or comment on my part, the good lady has stated explicitly that she doesn't want a nightdress this year, but some garden implement called (I think) a whipper-clipper-snipper. I would appreciate your best advice on an appropriate compromise and, indeed, on the whole issue of Christmas presents.
Perplexed

Oh, come now. After 26 nighties, I think your wife is entitled to call a definite halt to proceedings. Pink flannelette nighties are, of course, indispensable for those days when you're too crook to get out of bed. Flimsy things may have other uses. But 26 of the things seem quite enough to be getting along with. The joy of giving is in trying to please the other person. So if she wants a garden implement, I think it is a trifle churlish of you to insist on a compromise. If funds are your problem, then I suggest you discuss it. If you can afford her heart's desire, I don't quite see your quandary.

Dear Kaz,
I have just gone out in the big world of house sharing. I share a three-bedroom cottage with three other girls. We get on well, but a few things bother me regarding the financial side of it. We divide into three the rent, gas, electricity and the phone. I hardly use the phone because my family lives close by, but one girl is forever on the phone.

The last account was a shock. I think we should note what calls we have on a pad by the phone, don't you? We buy our own food, but share coffee, tea, toilet paper, detergent, etc. Since I have been here (three months) I seem to have constantly done the buying. I feel that a tin for weekly donations to buy these things should be provided. They earn more than me (at the moment). One girl lent a blouse of mine to a friend without asking me first. I was cross about that. What rules do you recommend for house sharing?

Sharing

1. There shalt be no lending, borrowing or otherwise trying on of frocks and the like without permission.

2. Gas-baggers shalt be responsible for their own calls, and a chart shalt be kept. Shouldst someone seem to be cheating, Telecom charge an unnecessary fee for a list of calls made, which will arrive with the bill.

3. Unless everyone is pitching in fairly, there shalt be a kitty established.

4. Shirkers of the dishes shouldst know better and may be made to scrub the toilet.

5. A house meeting may be called by any member of the household who has at least two things to whinge about.

6. Thou shalt not bring home friends who think people with 'positive energy' will be 'successful' and who make undue smalltalk about dolphins or property prices.

7. Shouldst thou be a Kate Bush fan, thou shalt never inflict this on the rest of the household.

Dear Kaz,
I realise you cannot always direct your attention to the more profound issues of life. However, I hope you try to resolve these questions that reach to the core of human relationships. When the gilt has gone off the gingerbread, as they used to say in the classics, or the first bloom has gone off the relationship, there appears to be a proportionate loss in effective communications. One tends not to hear important

71

messages such as 'Put out the cat', 'It's the garbo's day tomorrow' or 'Robbo and Jane are coming over on Saturday'. This failure is not one-sided. As I sometimes say to my partner, 'You never listen to a thing I say'. Repetition leads to domestic discord. Kaz, is there a simple technique either partner may use, short of rudeness or physical assault, to ensure the message is received and understood? Is there some trick that will make the alarm bells ring, when one's beloved says something of import to the stability of the relationship? Is the price of domestic harmony eternal vigilance?

Shell-Shocked

The problem with longer-term relationships is that eventually the two partners spend less than 22 hours a day gazing adoringly at each other and saying 'That's exactly how I feel about it too. That's amazing'. Couples begin to have conversations while she is wrestling with the fanbelt under the hood, while the TV is on, while he is reading an autobiography of Grace Kelly. A possible way around the impasse is for each partner to wait for a response so the message is obviously received. Some may wish to say 'Affirmative' or 'Roger' but they will eventually grow out of it. Especially if one of you is called Roger. Boring old stuff like garbage nights should be put on a calendar and allocated as a chore, otherwise it never gets remembered. That way nobody can say later, 'I told you' or 'Why didn't you just do it yourself?'. If I was an American psychologist, I'd tell you that you need 'quality time' and a program of interface networking skills. But all I can really say is that eye contact makes a lot of difference. Try it for a while. If it doesn't work, let me know.

Dear Kaz,
My wife is still annoyed with me for not recognising International Women's Day, but I don't know the appropriate way to celebrate it. I don't want to get it wrong again next year.

Cad

Oh, well, never mind. You're supposed to notice the achievements of women; remember that women do 70 per cent of the world's work and own one per cent of its wealth. Reassess your share of the housework, that kind of thing. There is absolutely no need to swan about the place saying you're a committed male feminist and failing to notice the dishes in the sink, as this makes most women feel extremely nauseated. It is

72

a little-known fact that the day after International Women's Day is designated Short, Fat, Grumpy Men's Day. As in all matters of etiquette, one just has to be reasonable. 'Happy International Women's Day my friend, would you like smoked salmon and scrambled eggs in bed and a video featuring Dennis Quaid for breakfast?' is a good start.

Dear Kaz,
During Easter I went bushwalking with my friend in the Bogong High Plains. During our walk we rounded a corner and saw a most disturbing sight. A man had fallen into a creek, the seat of his trousers was wet and so were his boots; as well he had gashed his forehead on a rock and looked extremely disconsolate. His wife was standing on the bank, assisting him up. When she saw us, she said, 'Look at my stupid husband'. Is it right for the man's wife to embarrass him like that?

Wondering

His wife will do more than embarrass him if she finds out he's been traipsing around the high plains with a quick-thinking woman . . . if it really was his wife, perhaps it was extremely rude, perhaps it was his just desserts. I can't tell.

Dear Kaz,
I share with three others and keep finding unwanted hairs when I go to shower. How should I handle this delicate problem?

Hair Today, Gone Tomorrow

I think I'll have to split your question. Firstly, if you are finding unwanted hairs, you may be going through adolescence. This is a perfectly normal thing and nothing to worry about. Large companies make squillions of dollars by convincing people to remove post-adolescent hair with electricity, chemicals or sharp blades. You could try one of those. Secondly, if you are referring to other people's hairs in the shower recess, you can leave a polite note on the fridge suggesting that there be a roster for cleaning the bathroom, or you can close your eyes while showering. Some members of the Catholic clergy recommend this as a matter of course. Mind the soap.

Dear Kaz,
I feel my wife's essential niceness is being eclipsed by the demands of a leaking roof, crying baby and my domestic habits. I wonder if you have any words of advice for my wife (or rather, I must admit, de facto) and I who are both anxious to keep ourselves nice in difficult circumstances.

Perturbed

Fix the roof, help with the baby and stop leaving damp, scrunched-up towels in the fridge.

Dear Kaz,
I have always tried to keep myself 'nice' but recently I have moved into a house with two men who are lovely and caring kinda guys, but these two co-habitators of mine have a rather indelicate problem. They shed pubic hair in the shower, which is above the bath. I do enjoy a bath, but it has become extremely tiresome cleaning up before my weekly soak. How do I broach this sensitive subject with them?

Concerned And Caring Co-habitator
North Balwyn

You are not really from North Balwyn, but I have changed your suburb for reasons I shall explain later. The editor of this column may pale at this letter and scurry off to see if it fits into the family newspaper sensibilities from the style council, but it must be a serious problem because since I began this column this is the fourth letter seeking help in this regard. I suggest you cut out this letter and response and sticky-tape it to the fridge. Shared households everywhere will be doing it, and your anonymity will be preserved. Underline this bit: PLEASE LEAVE THE BATH CLEAN AFTER YOUR SHOWER. More drastic action may include tantrums when they are entertaining, or a collection of the offending items (with tweezers) placed in an envelope and mailed to the offender.

THE NEXT WEEK:

The mailbag this week has been chock-a-block with pubic hair, following last week's advice. One correspondent accuses me of being chauvinist about men, another asks how to tell the difference between chest hair and pubic, and another claims that moulting is 'the adult male mating sign'. I hardly

74

imagined that this distasteful subject would arouse so much emotion on the part of readers. I hope I make myself entirely clear when I say this is not a sexual matter, it is an issue of cleanliness. And you all know where the Wettex is.

Dear Kaz,
My husband and I recently went up to Queensland for a holiday. We are in early retirement. On arriving at our friends' house for a two-day visit, we were told all was planned for us. My husband was taken out fishing each day by the man of the house in his boat, seeing the islands. The woman of the house took me to all the new, nearby shopping complexes and on visits to her friends where we sat and drank cups of tea and chatted about recipes, shopping, grandchildren, etc. I would far rather have gone fishing . . . I asked at one morning tea whether they were concerned about the environment and saving all their beautiful rainforests and waters in the area and they looked at me as though I had come from outer space. So Kaz, are they as I should be in my 60s? Or can I go on being me (and a bit odd, I gather)?

The Odd One

Hosts should always present a range of options for guests to choose from. Otherwise, animal liberationists may be taken to the zoo; claustrophobics booked into cave-exploring; and abseiling octogenarians roped into macrame. You know the answer about being yourself; it's better than being beside yourself. Reach an understanding with your husband so next time if you say, 'Fishing sounds great', he'll support you. Otherwise, consider separate holidays.

To Cold Feet: It is neither the man's nor the woman's job to warm up the sheets for a partner. The polite thing to do is to take responsibility for one's own hot-water bottle.

Dear Kaz,
I have a problem: my live-in-boyfriend of several years finds some of my friends (and especially some of their partners) to be real bores, and doesn't want to socialise with them. I'm quite happy to go out with them or visit them alone, but when it comes to more formal occasions (weddings, dinner parties, etc) I think it's reasonable to expect

my boyfriend to make the odd appearance. Am I just being selfish? Should I tell my friends he thinks they're a pack of bores? I have no desire to ditch him and I get on perfectly well with his friends.

Confused

One should not attend a wedding unless one is fully prepared to be happy about being there. Likewise, one should not attend a dinner party if one is likely, at any stage, to sulk. Your boyfriend should be left to his own devices. But remember this when he wants you to cook for his boss, attend the greyhound fanciers' barbecue or talk to any of his relatives. Don't tell your friends what he thinks of them. No doubt they think he's a snob, or terribly mysterious. If you ever marry the bloke, you are within your rights to demand his presence at the wedding. Whatever you do, don't lose your friends just because he doesn't like them. They may well last longer in your affections.

Dear Kaz,
I am a lady of middle years. If I doubled my age I would be in the *Guinness Book of Records*. Two problems trouble me about house-guests. We live in the country and seem to have hordes who travel to their ultimate destination via wherever in the state we happen to live! Whose responsibility is it to say when it is time to retire for the night? Does the hostess say, 'I'm pooped, must go to bed', or does one wait for the relaxed guest to finish watching his or her favourite late-night show or to tell that last, long anecdote? Problem two: how does one deal with the guest who sits down to a meal (over which one has slaved mentally and physically) and then proceeds to recount her own adventures in the culinary acts or those of others that she has sampled? I find this quite disconcerting. I am saving paper, hence writing on each side, so I must not start another page.

Hostie

Go to bed the very minute you feel like it and eschew the last anecdote. Your second problem is a little more difficult. If this is perpetrated by one particular houseguest, do not invite them again. They invite themselves, you say? When they ring to advise you of their imminent arrival, you may say, 'Oh, how dreadful, I am afraid we cannot have any visitors then'. No explanation is necessary and do not be badgered into making up an excuse. They just turn up on the doorstep, you say? Two options here: grab a coat and say, 'Oh lovely to see you but why didn't you ring? I'm just off—I've just poisoned the entire house with terrible chemicals to get rid of the rat plague. I hope it works this time!', and shut the door firmly behind you. Alternatively, recommend a local hotel for them. If all else fails, gently interrupt their foodie reverie with a description of how the local abattoir does its stuff, or the more intricate preparations (from scratch) of haggis or tripe. Bon appetit!

Dear Kaz,
My 16-year-old sister has thick, black hair and when she has a shower she leaves the soap embalmed in it. I occasionally beg her to clean up any members of her cranial community that have been emancipated during the course of her bathus verticulus, but to not avail. Would you opine a nice solution to my conundrum?
Funky Cold Kahuna

This is the ninth letter on the same subject since January 1989. May I suggest you use your own soap? If it is the unsightly nature of the matter that concerns you, you could provide your sister with a little tin to keep her soap in.

To Wondering: If I were your husband I would be pretty annoyed about the bathroom being draped in dental floss, too. For heaven's sake get yourself a floss-in-progress tin with a lid so he doesn't have to look at it and you can get on with more pressing issues. Nationalising the banks is a good one; heaps of opportunity for discussion there, I should think.

To Peeved: Your wife is right, you are wasting my time. Luckily, that is one of my favourite pursuits in the cause of 'Keep Yourself Nice'. If your wife wishes that you do not read to her with a mouthful of apple, I suggest you comply. I'm glad domestic bliss seems to have settled over your little nest and trust that you have stopped leaving wet towels everywhere. How's the baby?

Dear Kaz,
Pray tell what topic the conversation might turn to during a television commercial for tampons. Do we really need these advertisements, or should we be aiming for conversation to be abandoned altogether?
Irritated But Not Embarrassed

This reminds me about the joke concerning the man who wanted a box of tampons so he could go swimming and horseriding anytime he chose. I suggest you get up and announce you are going to make a cup of tea, as soon as the ad comes on. Reel off a long list of options from Earl Grey to Rosehip and go through all the lemon/honey/sugar/milk options. If the ad is repeated 47 times during the course of the program, this is going to wear a bit thin. Otherwise, turn the sound down during all the commercials and conduct quizzes about the program. 'Will Krystal twig to the dastardly plot before the next ad break?' 'What colour dress was Matron wearing in the back paddock scene?'

8. UNCLE HAROLD IS THICKER THAN WATER

UNCLE ERN DOES THE DANCE OF
THE SEVEN Y-FRONTS DURING DINNER

It's all relative; elderly aunts with fixations; mother says 'no' best; no children aloud; flighty grandmas.

Very few of us are born without a tummy button or relatives, but that doesn't mean we have to be fond of them. Even when we are fond of them, there are inevitably problems. Should it be an 'innie' or an 'outtie'; is it all right to use cotton buds during the ablution process; what is the difference between lint and fluff?

Relatives, too, can pose social difficulties. Despite the best efforts of fiction writers in the policy department of most major political parties in what passes for a democracy: MOST FAMILIES DO NOT CONSIST OF A FATHER WITH A HOLDEN, A MOTHER WITH A WETTEX IN ONE HAND AND TWO BLONDE CHILDREN DEAD KEEN ON CONSUMER GOODS. Cut this out and send it to them if you think it'll do any good.

No, families are more often made up of Great Aunty Ollie who can never find her teeth and addresses all male visitors to the house in Lithuanian proverbs; Uncle Ern who likes to frighten dinner party guests with stirring performances of the Dance Of The Seven Y-fronts; fathers-in-law who run white-gloved hands over anything stationary; mothers-in-law who demand that dinner conversation be restricted to the battle strategy of the latter half of the Somme campaign between March and Spring of 1917; toddlers who ask, 'Do penguins have oral sex?' when being introduced to elderly members of the clergy; and cousins called Craig who take Morris Minor engines apart in the kitchen.

Sometimes, this leads to tension.

The general rule with the doddering faction is to feign tolerance and treat them with respect. This can have its advantages, as it is harder to conduct a blazing argument with somebody who has not turned on their hearing-aid since Labor tried to nationalise the banks. When my own great-grandmother got to the stage of serving caterpillar sandwiches and accusing her 93-year-old boyfriend of playing the field, my father was often called in as an adviser on criminal matters. Somebody was stealing her corsetry and the finger of suspicion was pointed somewhat shakily at Meals On Wheels. The jewellery had been sewn into the bottom of the curtains in the front room to prevent similar light-fingered affrontery. Dad managed to convince her not to call the local constabulary, after which she remarked kindly that her grandson was 'So nice, almost like one of the family'.

We all feel like that about relatives sometimes.

The main problems seem to occur when it appears that a relative is trying to control one's life, never mind if one is 43 and lives in another state. Here it is a matter of tact. If Aunty Merle asks you every time you see her why you haven't found a husband yet, it inevitably will pall as a great joke after the first 11 years or so. Bright, casual ways of fobbing off the question in the early years can be adopted, as in, 'It's early days yet', or 'I'm quite happy thankyou', or 'Have you met my room-mate, Big Marlene?'. One must make one's own decision about whether to change to 'Get outta my face, Aunty Merle', or simply adopt a more discerning approach to accepting invitations to family gatherings.

Generally, one ought to treat the members of one's own family with the same respect and good manners reserved for anybody else. This means that if one would not strike a passing salesperson a glancing blow to the side of the head with a length of cable because the salesperson mispronounced 'oliagenous' one ought not to lay about members of the family with a rolled up newspaper with a cricket bat in it just because they have collectively and unanimously voted against your brown cardigan.

Family members must learn that however hard they try, they are not likely to transform the personal habits of somebody who has reached the voting age. Younger children, however, are another matter. Their parents or guardians have responsibility for them on social occasions, and letting them run completely amuck, or worse, amok, is simply not on, unless that is the desired effect.

I know of one family which cautioned its children sternly on the doorstep before entering somebody else's home. 'And remember, kids, RINSO', one of the adults would say. RINSO stands for 'Right Inside, No Showing Off'. Another family adopted FHB—Family Hold Back—for those occasions when there may not be enough food to go around and the guests had first choice. Parents would do well to ensure that their feral children do not ruin their chances of being invited anywhere but the principal's office.

In these days of what the Americans call—rather violently for students of kitchen gadgetry—the blended family, even more embroiling social situations can crop up, involving three stepmothers, nephews with chronological seniority over aunts, and rafts of cousins removed once too often.

They all deserve no more, no less consideration than members of the public. And they have an obligation to be polite and tolerant of you.

Unless you are Craig.

Dear Kaz,
I have had a lover for the past year and recently introduced her to my wife and kids. We are now all 'family friends'. After I flirted with another woman, my wife's best friend, she unfortunately thinks she loves me. This woman is also now good friends with my lover. I love my lover very much, my kids very much, my wife a little and her best friend not at all. The problem is we are all going camping and it could get out of hand. What do I do?

Camping

Gee, I love riddles. I don't know, let me guess. Maybe you're an engineer. Or, you might be a rigger or a bank clerk. OK, I give up. Write, and let us know.

He didn't.

Dear Kaz,
My elderly aunty has invited me to a small party at her home. The thing is, I know she is trying to introduce me to some people who will have a 'good influence' upon me. I really like my aunty, despite the fact that she's a bit potty. She's into a very strict religion, and wants me to join. Should I go, as I have absolutely no intention of 'joining' or remaining polite in the face of their missionary position?
Reluctant

Don't go, it will only upset your aunty. And if you did convert, she'd only have to find somebody else. While you're around, at least she has a project.

Dear Kaz,
I require your assistance upon a point of etiquette. While my friend and I are undressing each other preparatory to making love, she insists that all items of clothing should immediately be neatly folded or placed on hangers. She is adamant that this is what her mother taught her. I maintain that my mother always advised me that true politeness lay in giving one's undivided attention to one's companion, and would prefer to leave our clothing to fall unheeded to the floor. Can you please advise us why we seem to be thinking of them at such a time?
The Man With White Cat Hairs On His Dark Suit

Undressing seems rather popular this week. I suppose it makes an interesting change from fashion. Here's a shocking thought: mothers are not always right. Except mine, of course, who is presently trying to save Port Melbourne from what seem to be, in our opinion, rapacious developers and dubious toxic waste. But I digress. Feel free to hurl your strides around the boudoir with abandon, but let your friend do it her way, too. As to why you are thinking of your mothers at such time, I most certainly don't know. You may both have massive guilt complexes or just be strangely distracted during moments of etiquette dilemma. Many people are.

Dear Kaz,
My sister, a science graduate, has yet to find work. After months of job hunting she has become gloomy and reclusive, spending each day locked in the laundry with sinister-looking chemicals, gas bottles and strange glass-ware. I can't introduce her to nice young men (who would

83

support her) because she always gets around in goggles, rubber gloves and old overalls, smelling like chemicals. How can I stop her blowing up the suburb, destroying the ozone layer and driving away suitors?

Oh Brother

Leave your sister alone, unless you need to do a load of washing. It sounds to me like she is a photographer or a perfumier or is discovering a cure for centralised power, all perfectly respectable occupations for a young gel. Imagine how awful it would be if she were dating young National Party members and the house smelled of sheep and hypocrisy. If your suburb, incidentally, is North Balwyn, consider buying her some nitroglycerine for her birthday.

Dear Kaz,
Before I left home my mother made me promise never to scoop my peas and never walk through the park at night, but now I do both things. Do you think it is wrong to disregard my promise? Should I tell her?

Asziz

Yes. No. It is very wrong of you to make a promise you cannot keep. But I'll tell you what. I'll let you off the pea charge if you have self-defence lessons. If you keep walking through parks alone at night, it's going to be the police who end up telling your Mum you didn't keep your promise. And they have no choice but to visit in the middle of the night, bringing grief instead of calling cards.

Dear Kaz,
My mother keeps knitting me jumpers, and I hate them all. I appreciate the thought, but I can only wear them when I go to see her. The other day I was on my way there and somebody I know saw me wearing the most hideous one. What can I do?

Aldo

They say a stitch in time saves nine, Aldo, and although it makes absolutely no sense to me, I suspect if you don't speak up soon you will be awash in dubious, fairisle, cable-knit monstrosities. I don't know whether you or your mum have thought about this, but there are some people in this country who get so cold and scared at night they sleep in rubbish bins or in little corners of public buildings. Perhaps you should tell your mum it would make you really happy if she could knit some things for the Salvation Army or the Brotherhood of St Laurence. That way, she can vary her repertoire and also make some things for kids, instead of big jumpers for a son who doesn't choose his own patterns. But don't hurt her feelings. Tell her you have enough lovely jumpers. Perhaps it's a project you could undertake together. She'd probably really like that.

Dear Kaz,
Can you please suggest a way out of a difficult situation? We've accepted an invitation that says 'no children allowed'. We like our kids and we so rarely get an invitation, that we want everyone to go.
Puzzled Parents

What kind of a function is this? Nude mud-wrestling? Ian Sinclair's home movies? If so, maybe this is not appropriate for tots. There is also the possibility that the behaviour of your children in public is the reason for so few invitations. But perhaps not many people are fond of children, preferring to invest in white shagpile carpet. Such people resent the intrusion of children at social functions and resent extrusions on the shagpile. It can be quite disconcerting to discuss Serbian politics while somebody is weeing on your trousers. If a host does not wish children to attend a function, he or she should explain in person or over the telephone the reason for this. 'No children allowed' on an invitation can be offensive. Having already accepted the invitation, however, you should go. If you don't care about repercussions, dress the children as short merchant bankers and introduce them as a visiting delegation from Omsk. They will enjoy it.

Dear Kaz,
My sister-in-law, who is married to my elder brother (a member of the North Balwyn Rotary Club) refuses to participate in any discussions I initiate if any mention of my expensive overseas travel happens to arise—which normally occurs within a minute or two of the conversation being struck . . . How can I bring up the subject of my very frequent round-the-world trips without seeming to be common, boorish and hoydenish?
Frequent Flier

The *Macquarie Dictionary* defines hoyden as an ill-bred girl or tomboy, and hoydenish as boisterous. There is nothing wrong with being boisterous, but you are simply a Rotarian-Baiter. May I suggest a window seat in an electrical storm?

Dear Kaz,
I am 67-years-old and have just one problem. I met a very nice man recently at the bowls club and as we are both widowed, have had some lovely outings together. We have separate houses and don't want to live together, but we planned a nice holiday together on the Gold Coast. To keep costs down, we booked the same room. My children, who are all married themselves, are horrified. They say he's probably a dirty old man and I should know better at my age. But he's very nice. He's even offered to pay half my ticket because I don't have as much money as he. Please answer this letter, but I will only sign myself.

Oldie

Now you listen to me. You jolly well go to the Gold Coast and have a particularly splendid time. Too old for it, indeed! Perhaps your children are very busy people and haven't had time to think it through. If this little holiday will make you happy, and you fully trust this fellah of yours, then you don't have a problem at all. Your children have a problem. I don't know whether you will have, or have had, intimate relations (if I may be so bold), but I don't see why not, unless he's been hot-footing it around town without a condom. You don't want syphilis at your age; it'll keep you off the beach for half a day at least. Try to explain things to your offspring. If they still don't understand, then go ahead and have fun anyway. I bet they didn't always do what they were told, hmm?

Here's a happy ending to the letter published recently from the couple I advised to carry out their plans for a fab holiday despite the disapproval of the lady's 'grown-up' children. I don't know if it's a genuine letter but I like it anyway:

Dear Kaz,
Thank you for the fearless advice you gave 'Oldie'. The Gold Coast holiday was a smash hit, crowned by my runaway victory in the invitational singles at the Burleigh Heads bowling club, to say nothing

of a few minor triumphs off the rink, as it were. Shouting Mollie half the price of her ticket turned out to be a wise investment, as we have now revised our earlier decision not to live together, and I move into her two-storey next week. My mildewed weatherboard within hiking distance of the shopping centre goes on the market shortly after, if any of your readers are interested. As for the possibility of dangers caused by 'hot-footing it around town without a condom', I gave that up after a nasty, but mercifully brief, experience in Cairo that robbed me of the chance to participate at El Alamein. My only problem is Mollie's insistence of wearing rather sharp-edged curlers on retiring, and there are occasions when I am fearful of irreversible injury.

Colin

By my calculations Colin must be getting on a bit. He must be a truly exceptional bowler.

Dear Kaz,
My stepfather wants me to call him dad, but I don't feel comfortable about it. I already had a dad. I don't know what to do. My mum says it's up to me.

Offspring

Tell your mum how you feel and enlist her help in talking to your step-dad. It is perfectly OK for you to use his first name, if he doesn't mind. If you explain politely, with regard for his feelings, your step-dad should understand. If he has a sense of humour, tell him you really wanted to call him Baldy, but you will settle for Bruce.

Dear Kaz,
I hope you can help me with a problem I have about a Christmas present of perfume given to me by an elderly aunt. As I read the label of the perfume, I saw that it was propelled by CFCs. This aunt, at the age of 85, has just discovered that it is nice to give presents at Christmas (Editor's note: or that you are finally nice enough to give presents to) and I think it would hurt her feelings if I pointed out that using her present would be an act of environmental vandalism. I don't think she would understand a connection between my perfume, a hole in the ozone layer over Antarctica and skin cancer. I thought

I might send the perfume back and tell them to get their act together, and just avoid the question if my auntie ever asked. What do you think?

Unscented Greenie

I think you should have exchanged the present weeks ago, but it's probably too late for that. Tell your aunt everything. It will make for an interesting discussion. Buy her membership of Greenpeace, the Australian Conservation Foundation, or a similar organisation. Get her a copy of the Commission for the Future's guide for personal action to help save the planet (cheap, recycled paper, at newsagents). She's cluey enough to buy you a present, so don't assume she's loopy just yet.

To Eternally Platonic: Big deal if most of your male friends are gay. Does it matter about the sexual preferences of your women friends? Who cares? Not me. Or you either if you're a real friend. Do you always introduce friends to your relatives on the basis of whether they are husband-prey or just platonic friends? It's none of your relatives' business anyway. If they actually come out and say, 'Are you and Brad going to get married?', you can say 'No'. You don't have to mention Trent at all. Why your friends are an impediment to meeting straight men I cannot imagine, unless your first question to all and sundry is, 'In a nutshell, what are your sexual preferences?' instead of, 'Hello, how are you?'

9. SAY WHAT?

Mind your language; bonking; spinsters; gentlemen; the C-word; frocks versus gowns; tongue-tied.

According to Ita Buttrose's *A Guide To Modern Etiquette*, one of my moderately well-thumbed reference tomes, to say it with flowers, and here I speak of African marigolds, is to suggest vulgar minds. And more: a yellow carnation may well earn you a slap in the kisser, a red carnation quaintly ejaculates, 'Alas for my poor heart!', the cyclamen denotes diffidence, the dahlia instability. To give a decent bunch of hydrangeas is to cast some pretty hefty aspersions (not nasturtiums) on one's character, and tuberoses are practically indecent.

Now, I tell you this not because I want you to rush the local library for Ita's full list (page 135 *ibid*) but to illustrate, rather graphically and with a heady fragrance of warning lingering in the still night air and so forth, that you have to be very careful what you say, most particularly when you haven't the faintest idea what it means.

One must tailor one's speech for the audience. For example, it is no good saying, 'Below the poverty line—heaps of them' to a Treasurer, as they will only look blank and become upset. When in Rome, one must speak in Italian or at least learn the word *gabinetti* or be fated to be caught short almost constantly.

So what are the modern uses of the English, or in our case, Australian language, which so plague people these days? What are the syllables which trip us up, send us sprawling across the gerunds and leave us scrabbling blindly on the turf for a serviceable preposition?

The issues enunciated by the readers of the column were, as they say in the manuals explaining how to erect a do-it-yourself banana lounge, many AND varied. And I can't say this shocked me. Ours is a living language. A living, breathing, robust, pert sort of a language with definite rules about how it wishes to be used. For example, a married couple cannot by definition have a love-nest, nor indeed a sex romp. Television reporters, to single out a sliver of society, are continually telling us that somebody has had a bit of a demise, when they are just trying to tell us that somebody got the pink slip in the pay-packet. Thus, many families watching the six o'clock bulletin have been given a bit of a jolt, under the impression that a loved one had been snatched up to glory when in fact they have only lost their seat or had the richard in an employment sense. We all have our pet hates, and correspondents to the column are no exception in this regard.

They have bravely stepped into the fraying edges of language and posed questions such as, 'Where did the word "bonking" come from?'. In the great tradition of 'Keep Yourself Nice' other readers hurled themselves at their stationery and fired off at least fourteen entirely incompatible and utterly believable etymological explanations. That's the kind of experience this is.

Others have inquired as to the propriety of the words 'spinster' and 'gentleman', the subtle and distinctive differences between a 'frock' and a 'gown', how to address others at parties, whether it's okey-dokey to tell huge pork pies to total strangers and how to differentiate between 'nauseous' and 'nauseating' (vital).

Just for those not within cooee of a local library I shall here paraphrase some of Ita's definitions of the sentiments expressed by certain floral varieties:

- Azalea: It's time you went on the wagon again.
- Columbine: What a berloody stupid thing to do.
- Yellow carnation: You complete mongrel.
- Striped carnation: Not likely, sunshine.
- Jonquil: How about it, then, eh?
- Peony: I am prostrate with mortification.
- Scarlet poppy: You little ripper.
- Yellow tulips: Let's just put our hearts in the blender now and save ourselves the middle bit of romance.

So, if language is proving a tall order, say it with flowers but don't forget to duck.

Dear Kaz,
While talking to a boring chappie at a party, is it all right to lie and
make up wonderful stories about who you are and what you've done?
They wouldn't be lies . . . more like creative answers to his boring
questions. Wouldn't they?

Patsy

What is the poor man supposed to say: 'Wrestled an anaconda lately?'
Party small talk can be excruciating—but at least he was interested in
you, as well as himself. But if he's so boring, you'll tell him at the punch
bowl that you are a reincarnation of Marie Antoinette undertaking research
into alfalfa, and then not recognise him under the Hills Hoist as you
regale him with your insistence that you are an exotic dancer of Serbian-
Tongan lineage. If you do feel able to invent wild stories, do it well and
have fun, but make sure the other person knows that it is all in fun.
Incidentally, some people will always pursue you, even if you make up
DULL stories about yourself.

ON NAUSEA:

Granny Two and Ernest Pedant have each written to correct my grammar
on a point of order. Instead of saying I was 'nauseous' because of some of
the letters lately, I should have admitted to being 'nauseated'. In Ernest Pedant's
opinion, this misuse of the word has been perpetuated by frequent proclamations
by somebody called Marcia Brady, although why I am being taken to task
for being ungrammatical by somebody who watches the TV series 'The Brady
Bunch' enough to discern a trend is rather beyond me. Granny Two was
more acceptably sycophantic enough to say, 'I'm sure you are never nauseous'.
Ha.

Dear Kaz,
Recently I went to a social event (sort of like a party) where I met
an attractive stranger who seemed unattached and also looked
interesting. Unable to speak to this person alone that evening, the
following day I rang and asked the question, 'Are you married, engaged,
or in love?' After recognising my voice and laughing, the answer came
back, 'Well, yes I am, actually'. The conversation ended and I expected
to hear no more. The following evening I went to another social event
(a party) that was very crowded and at which I thought I knew no

one. After a long period of obligatory party chat, I heard my name being called. I turned to see the person I'd hoped I'd never see again, talking to someone I knew and whom I now realised must be a mutual friend. They were looking at me and laughing. Trying to disappear out the back door, I felt an arm on my shoulder and heard a whisper in my ear. 'I hear you've been a sleazebag!' I turned in horror to see another friend gloating at my obvious embarrassment. I left. Since that time, every person I have spoken to greets me with laughter and a smirking, 'I hear what you've been up to'. Kaz, what should I do? Should I fight the insinuations head on, or should I ignore them? And of the attractive stranger; I am angry and hurt that I have been misrepresented on the basis of a (reasonably) innocent phone call. Should I let the person know how I feel?

Embarrassed, Sleepless, And House-Bound

Excuse me if I'm a little confused. If you obtained this person's telephone number from another party (so to speak), perhaps you should have asked the other party if the 'attractive stranger' was married, in lerv, or attached, heterosexual, homosexual, a coffee drinker, etc. If, on the other hand, you knew enough about this person to telephone, or perhaps it was given to you by this person at the (sort of) party . . . it's VERY confusing, I must say. I suppose you might look for some new friends who don't carry on quite so much. It seems, however, that you will have to brazen it out. It was extremely unfair of the 'attractive stranger' to spill the beans. If things go on like this, we're not going to be game to speak to anybody at a party. Maybe that's why the music's so loud sometimes. If you decide to brazen it through, take the honest road: you didn't do anything outrageous. There is no problem. You express some concern that your friends will read the letter. It sounds like they haven't got anything much better to do. Good luck.

ON BONKING:

Dear Kaz,

I was surprised at your recent use of the word 'bonking' which is generally used by the most down-market magazines. What would you suggest is the most appropriate expression for a well-brought-up gentleman (or lady) to use when inviting a member of the opposite sex to engage in sexual congress?

Completely Bonkers

'Bonking' is used by headline writers because it's short and not considered obscene. In answer to your question, members of any gender inviting members of any other gender for a spot of non-specific ferreting in the nether regions need not feel compelled to use any specific words in the way of description. The only compulsory mentions in this department are 'safe sex', 'condoms' and the like. When refusing such an invitation, one must consider the way in which the question was posed. One may then answer, 'I'd rather kiss a dog' or, 'I'm flattered but I'd really rather not'.

Dear Kaz,
Could you provide your readers with a brief history of the word 'bonk' and its evolution to the present status of describing what us humans enjoy doing the most?

A Little Worried

I'm afraid you have the wrong end of the stick. 'Bonking' does not refer to eating cold chocolate biscuits in front of an open fire at all, it refers to, as one reader would have it, 'sexual congress'. As far as I know it is an English word with English synonyms of 'boffing' and 'rogering'. Perhaps a university student, linguist or sheet-metal worker might have some more information. If they write to me, I'll pass it on.

Dear Kaz,
In 1969, archaeologists discovered a cave just outside the south-east Chinese town of Bonking that had an incredible collection of erotic paintings. The word passed into British slang via the Hong Kong correspondent of the 'Daily Mirror'.

Rob

Dear Kaz,
'Bonk' is a Dutch verb, according to the Van Dale dictionary. One of the meanings is a derogatory term for sexual congress.

John

Dear Kaz,
'Bonking' IS an English word, and comes from the sound, and nothing else. Because of the inclement English weather it is seldom possible to have sex outdoors, and the Mini and its ilk prevented the act from

94

occurring indoors except for the most agile among us. Thus, young lovers in search of sexual repose had no option but to drive to a secluded spot and commence their union upon the bonnet. Unfortunately, the designers at British Leyland had not considered such an event and subsequently the weight caused the bonnet to dent, producing a large 'bonk!'. The increasing popularity of bonking in Australia can be attributed to the number of small imported cars and the increased rainfall caused by the depletion of the ozone layer.

Station Wagon Preferred

Dear Kaz,

For 40 years or more my family has used the verb 'to bonk' to refer to an accidental thump, often to the head. Partridge's *Dictionary of Slang and Unconventional English* confirms that 'bonk' has a history of meaning 'a sharp blow' from at least the 1920s. Is it too late to put in a plea for readers to resist the McDonald's-isation of our language and use any of the hundreds of our own beaut words and phrases for horizontal folk dancing?

Ian

Dear Kaz,

The term 'bonk' originated with the introduction of bedsprings for commoners in the 19th Century. It is an onomatopoeic word simulating the sound the springs make while they are under some strain. When automobiles became the preferred venue for such human folly, the term became even more popular owing to the fact that there were more inanimate objects to strike, including ones that went 'HONK!'. The term was also popularised by the phrase, 'Things that go bonk in the night', which referred to noises after dark that frightened one during childhood. The current craze for such a silly word to refer to sexual congress stems from the enlightenment of many folk that it is indeed one of the most ludicrous of human pastimes. It has recently been discovered that persons who bonk compulsively manifest signs of dysfunction. This led to the phrase, 'utterly bonkers'. A thesis published this year by feminist neurophysiologist Professor Hildegarde L'Amour hypothesised that the traditional immaturity of males was caused in the missionary position. I hope this enlightens your readers.

No Bonks For Yonks

Well, now you know. 'Keep Yourself Nice' is now banning the subject of sexual congress and anything to do with it for at least five weeks. Fishing, cuddling, introductions, socks, almost anything else will do. Come to think of it, a very good letter about brown socks came in the mail last week, and I can only say I hadn't noticed they were no longer in the shops. I find it difficult to believe.

Dear Kaz,
Years ago, I gently rebuked my daughter by saying, 'Do be more tactful'. She then asked, 'What does tactful mean?'. I answered, 'You do not talk funerals at weddings and you do not talk weddings at funerals'. Two recent examples will better illustrate. A cleric's son said to me, 'What sort of a man have we leading us? An atheist'. Almost daily, people who take their leave say, 'God bless'. I have been an atheist for 40 years. What should I say to them? 'May the reason of Bertrand Russell go with you' or 'Seek daily knowledge from Ingersoll'? Perhaps I should force my unwanted views on others and presume I am mixing with atheists (figures published recently state 20 per cent of people are church attendees).

Unbeliever

As somebody said on Radio JJJ this week: 'It's Your Day, Don't Share It With A Christian'. We-e-ll, maybe that's a bit harsh. Just saying 'God bless' isn't too bad. It's better than, 'Hi, I'm Hank. That's my foot in the door and I'm going to share the word of our Lord with you this day'. I like both your suggestions, which seem to show you are a caring sort, although I was under the impression that Ingersoll makes orthopaedic footwear. You might say, 'Well, I'm blessed'. A man I met on the plane on my way to my brother's wedding this week told me: 'A little less tact now saves a lot of hurt later'. The man's name was Ron and he said the quote was from Ralph Waldo Emerson. At least he didn't talk about funerals.

Dear Madam,
I have been reading your little patch and now it seems you may be able to solve a very perplexing problem that has given my old age even more sting than usual. When I separated from a surrogate wife of some 20 years I became a non-practising heterosexual. At first I thought the condition was not only tolerable but permanent. At 50,

I have decided that I am really a spinster. The word is non-gender specific entirely but it will take some presentation to the public before it can be used by a non-practising heterosexual like myself on, say, the census form, without misunderstanding. I hope you can, in your way, introduce 'spinster' to general use by light-hearted banter.

Spinster

According to my dictionaries, a bloke can't be called a spinster unless his occupation is spinning, but don't let that stop you. 'Keep Yourself Nice' would welcome comments on this issue. Once I put my religion down on the census form as 'fashion' during a rare frivolous moment. I don't think the Government minds terribly. Good luck with the rest of your life, which I hope will give you opportunities to do some more practising whatever takes your fancy (safely). And don't call me Madam.

Dear Kaz,
I'm glad you attempted to stop 'Spinster' who described himself as a non-practising heterosexual, from unduly worrying. We all know what strain can do to one's 'practising' potential! He may be interested to know (if he hasn't already taken up spinning) that a bachelor, apart from being an unmarried man, was, historically, 'A young knight serving under another's banner'.

Grandma

Good on you, Gran. Does that make a 'bachelor flat' a place where nightly someone expects someone else to serve? (Hysterically).

Dear Kaz,
A spring blast. The word 'gentleman'!!! Once there were men, chaps, blokes, fellows. (I don't include guys. Un-Australian.) Now the word 'man' is almost a dirty word. We must say 'gentlemen' just like genteel, mid-Victorian days. What has come over us, who pride ourselves on everyone being equal and no class-consciousness or cultural cringe? Of all pretension and flagrant class distinction, 'gentlemen' takes first prize, considering some of the samples so designated. I hope you will agree, or you're no lidy (sic) either.

Contentious

97

Speaking of class-consciousness, mid-Victorians were more likely to call blokes 'coves'. The history that we read is mostly about the rich people, those with power. We don't see many mini-series about the starving waifs of London. Charles Dickens knew a lot more about it, but I digress. 'Guys' is a term favoured by young women, who only later in life come to describe men as 'boys' after the benefit of experience. The etiquette lesson is really to refer to people in terms they prefer.

Dear Kaz,
People who try to keep themselves nice should not be called silly names like Kaz. Nice people deserve nice names. Kaz is a fine name for a cat or a poodle, but not for people who want to keep themselves nice. Do you agree?

James

No. I believe it is only polite to address people by the names they have been given, or chosen for themselves. I am allergic to cats and my dog is called W.A.C.A. So do go and find yourself something useful to do, James old sausage.

Dear Kaz,
Some young men of my acquaintance, in moments of great distress, such as failing to sink the ball in a game of pool, are prone to use of the 'C' word (which I presume your paper won't print). As an anatomical description or in Scrabble, I personally find the word acceptable, but used as a term of abuse or in anger it upsets me. Despite knowing this, they continue to use it occasionally. Must I abandon the company of these young men entirely or would learning to beat them at pool be sufficient?

Linguistic Lament

Flog them at pool, thrash them at Scrabble and refuse to tolerate such language. If they do not comply, say, 'I've had a penis of a day', and go and find some new pool partners.

Dear Kaz,
Can you tell me in words of one cylinder (*sic*) what a 'frock' is? My sister and I always regard the word and its user as suspect. Is it a

dress? Why not say so? 'Frock' is rather Freudian, or twee, don't you think?

Dying To Know

A 'frock' is a day dress, and a 'gown' is an evening dress. These are lovely, evocative, old-fashioned words that do not deserve to be tossed out just because 'dress' is in vogue. It is a great shame that along with the drop-kick, many words are being lost to further generations, such as 'frock', 'crikey', 'ratbag' and 'rainforest'. I have not studied psychiatry myself, but frock-envy is a well-known condition, and I shouldn't be at all surprised if old Freudie had a floral fixation.

Dear Kaz,
Thank you for explaining the word 'frock', an old-fashioned dress, like the lovely old words like 'quid' and 'cripes' and 'loungeroom'. But my sister thinks a gown need not be for evening wear only, as she always wears one to the Melbourne Cup, even if it's just a good jumper and skirt. Hope you see her there, she looks very elegant.

Trendy

A gown is *not* a jumper and skirt. A gown is the sort of thing Grace Kelly wears while being chatted up by a young Cary Grant in a ballroom scene. I'm sure your sister looks splendid at the Cup. She could hardly do worse than the ornamental frails who hurl themselves in front of cameras with no regard for their own safety and who wouldn't know a fetlock from a forelock.

Dear Kaz,
I like to keep myself nice, but I terribly get tongue my tied. Last Saturday I went to my local hardware shop and asked: 'May I have a grip of Tarzan's tube, the stick that stuffs everything?', What I am to do? Please me help.

Tongue-Tied

Either you have been smoking marijuana on a regular basis for too long, or you are simply an entertaining person. Try thinking before you speak, but if you can't be bothered, never mind, hardly anyone does these days. It's hard enough getting some members of the more militarised branches of the police force to think before they shoot. Or economists to think before they make policy. What's the difference between bold and cheeky and bald and shirty anyway, life is short.

Dear Kaz,
Please settle an argument. My friend says 'dag' is a term of endearment, but I think it is a put-down. How about you?

Confused

I know people who can infuse the word 'darling' with unprecedented venom. Others can make 'rat's-breath' into an affectionate nickname. Generally, one is advised to stay away from such people, but you get my drift. Dagginess is in the eye of the beholder, and very often the preferred trouser style of the beholdee. Thus, it is perfectly clear. If you call your friend a dag, they may immediately cross you off their party list. If your friend calls you a dag, you can safely bask in the knowledge that you are held in high esteem.

Dear Kaz,
Cruising in my convertible Volkswagen last Friday, I was verbally assaulted by a group of young men with post-Holocaust hair cuts, who shouted at me, 'Yuppies Die!'. As a student of this column for several months now, and not wishing to be taken advantage of, I dutifully wound down my window and slagged all over their Ford Futura Fordomatic. I've since had reservations about this action, and wonder if you could advise me of a more acceptable protocol, should this unfortunate situation recur.

Jasmine

By jingo, I should think you'd have some reservations, too. What a disgraceful thing to do. You silly girl. You're lucky the bald lads didn't pile out of their motor car and eat your windscreen wipers. Spitting in broad daylight, honestly, I don't know what the world is coming to. It is possible that the young men mistook you for their friend Diana Yupp. They may have been mourning the death of their pet guppy. They may have been singing along to a song of the same name. Of course, they may also have been insulting you. So what? Don't you watch television? Haven't you read some political party policies? We are insulted all the time. And it's no cause for spitting. If you can't think up a piece of brilliant repartee, you may as well feign deafness.

My dear Miss or Mrs Cook (*sic*),
The honorific M/s has traditionally been used when the writer is unsure if the female recipient is in the maidenly or matronly state. In recent times, there has been a regrettable tendency to delete the oblique dash and mispronounce the result to rhyme with a diminutive of our gracious Queen's Christian name (*he means Liz*). **How do we overcome this abominable denigration of the Mother Tongue?**

Msogynist (*sic*)

Etiquette and good manners are all about respect for other people. To assume that the marital status of a woman is relevant is simply impertinent. If a woman has indicated a wish to addressed as 'Mrs', 'Miss', 'Ms', 'Mizz' or 'The totally fabulous', that is her choice. Take your 'Miss or Mrs Cook', for instance. You've misspelled it, for a start. And I don't think it's any of your business whether I am married or not. And neither does my husband. Or my girlfriend. If somebody wants to call themselves a misogynist, for example, I will not argue with it. You must be prepared for changes in a 'living language' otherwise we'd still be hither and thithering all over the place.

Dear Kaz,
How should I introduce my boyfriend? I am 44, he is 48, so boyfriend doesn't sound quite right. Lover is downright disgusting. We don't intend to get hitched, so I can't say fiancé, and simply saying friend won't warn other scheming females away from him.

Frank's Gal

Here are some options, not all of them recommended: (I'd like you to meet) my main squeeze; the like of my life; light of my loins; sweetheart; swain; or beau. You could try, 'I'd like you to meet Frank,' which, while pedestrian, is at least the most accurate thing you're likely to come up with. Don't forget to consider the extraordinarily remote possibility that nobody else is interested in him.

To Widowed: You may call yourself whatever you like, and so may your son. If he likes being called Junior, there's no reason to change, especially if it will confuse people in conversation. I take it you still want to be a Mrs. Whether you want to keep your husband's first name as your own is up to you. I have always been wary of the 'Mrs Bill Smith' solution,

101

as I think taking one name from a bloke is probably quite enough, and not having anything left of your own a trifle dismissive. Etiquette, however, dictates that you may call yourself Boadicea if you so desire, although don't blame the cousins if they keep forgetting. There's probably an old English rule about this, and I suspect it's to keep the husband's name. But we're not old and English, are we?

10. THE GRATING OUTDOORS

Golf and other perverts; street etiquette; on the beach; off the gardens; skiting on the wall.

Sooner or later you will have to face the outside world, even if it's just to stroll down to the corner milk bar for another tin of processed ravioli and some lime-flavoured dental floss in a non-aerosol pack. And so you will have to take some equipment with you.

If you have to negotiate any major mountainous crag effects, you would do well to have about your person some stout raffia, crampons, crimps and a working knowledge of knots used in the boating industry. Should you be required to ford a fjord, ice-picks, crampons, and a woolly hat might come in handy. Those in a National Party electorate know to venture out only when in possession of a full list of city council procedures, several unmarked bills in a brown paper bag and a full list of comments about a range of weather patterns.

Likewise, if one's journey takes one into the shadowy realm (panpipe music with those eerie cow bell bits here, thanks) of coming into contact with other people in the non-home type situation *per se*, as such, one must be prepared. Lord Baden-Powell was right. (A cold shower won't help, but that's a digression.)

Just as happy hikers have secreted a self-saucing pudding under the spare crimps, we must have a swag of etiquette knowledge along with us at all times, in case of emergency. Just as James Bond was bound to have a cigarette lighter in his left trousers pocket that actually produced a flame, as well as being a nerve-gas dispenser, Swiss Army knife, Clydesdale hoof-cleaning device and microwave oven, and hence was able to set off a smoke-detector in his hotel-room in a fit of pique upon finding himself with a long-legged Scandinavian lass who wasn't the slightest bit interested in him, we, too, must have our secret devices.

There is nothing more comforting in an emergency than a comprehensive working knowledge of good manners, and the correct way to behave. Unless it's having a large semi-automatic weapon the possession of which is illegal in the Northern Territory, Tasmania, the precincts of Nimbin and on Sundays in a Melbourne hardware store, and an uncle who's a QC.

You never know what will happen to you outside your own home, assuming that you have a home and have not been designated by the Government as an esteemed citizen of the world permitted by a special act of parliament to claim one blanket from the Salvos on the third Friday of each leap year with a publicly declared summer solstice isthmus zenith in Scorpio.

Yes, you never know what will happen to you—there's cheating on the golf course; men who don't know which side of the footpath to walk on and hence meander dangerously, and cause an obstruction to kiddy skateboarders looking for a bit of open slather; there are graffitists looking for a verb; lecherous and raucous beach-cricket players re-writing the definition of silly mid-on; and women in badly designed dresses emulating a parachuting demonstration in windy conditions described fairly accurately and somewhat relentlessly as blustery.

And of course, no outdoors selection would be truly complete without at least a curt nod in the direction of garden behaviour. Several women readers of a certain age have felt compelled, nay, driven, to write of their poignant plight at the hands (encased in hitherto pristine size-16 gardening gloves) of their newly-retired spouses. Deprived of a chance to don the overalls and stride forth with the spanner collection or wack on a tie and run for the train, these chaps with time, and sap, on their hands have taken to noticing the garden. No sooner have they realised that their yard is a whole new vista, the mower has been unleashed on the daphne bush and the pruning is launched with the sort of verve usually displayed by small children left in charge of a model of the Taj Mahal made from 7895 toothpicks. These women stand bereft in the centre of a scorched-earth policy implemented by men who have not done the research vis-à-vis the difference between the first daffodil of the season and a particularly troublesome patch of rampant choke-grass.

As a service to those women contemplating a new use for the poisons in the back shed shelved after reading the environment supplement in the 'Womens' Weekly', 'Keep Yourself Nice' has championed their cause. As with many responses to the problems of readers, a clipping from the column sticky-taped to the fridge can sometimes make a husband realise the danger of his actions before a second strike is mounted.

And remember—always carry some spare crampons in your handbag for emergencies.

Dear Kaz,
My husband has recently retired and after 41 years of living with him, I discover that he is a compulsive slasher, masher and mutilator of everything that gets in the way of his vigorous mowing. (Don't tell me to get him to BOWL—he's been doing that for 30 years.) All my asparagus are cut off at their socks, the lemon tree is looking poorly from frequent jabs at its base, my daisies are unable to flower, the lavender is gone, and the roses are all gone—he reckons they jump out at him. Our well-established apple tree had the misfortune to topple over in a storm. This tree had five grafts (Jonathon, Gravenstein, Granny Smith, Snow and another Delicious). It lay on the ground for months and had just begun to set its fruit. When I was out, he got busy and burnt it all up. It really has been a shock to me, because he helped me plan our garden and likes most living things. I'm sure we'll end up living in a fallow paddock similar to the Mallee farm from which I had my roots. What can I do?
Desperate

You poor darling. This is awful. It reminds me of the man across the road who comes out every morning and picks up the fallen petals on his neater-than-neat grass as if they were beer cans on the Buckingham Palace lawn. Your husband needs a jolly good tongue-lashing. You've known him for 41 years, so you know best whether to be sensible, wheedling, demanding, or threatening, or perhaps all of the above in ascending order. It cannot go on. Call a spade a decent implement and the mower out of bounds in designated areas. I showed your letter to a gardener, who burst into tears and muttered something about putting a stocking in the petrol tank of the motor-mower. You must make the nature-abuser realise that the garden is there for both of you, and joint decisions should be made about reaping and ripping. Can you get him interested in growing things instead of mowing things? Has he gone a bit tiddly and mistaken the garden for the bowling green? Can you get him interested in nature rambles at the Bot Gardens, or macrame, or bungy-jumping? Get his mind off slashing and burning. Good luck.

Dear Kaz,
Is it 'nice' to try and change someone? I live in the eastern suburbs (but I grew up in North Balwyn) and I have met a girl from the western suburbs. She likes pizza, I like expensive restaurants; she likes Southern Comfort, I like Grange. She even says 'youze'. However, as you have guessed, I am quite taken with her. Is there any hope? Should I be happy with 'one with the lot' and hard liquor or should I try to educate her?

East Meets West

Yeah, Yeah. You say potartoes and she says potatoes. Of course, there is always hope. Always. There will not always be an ozone layer, and integrity seems a bit out to lunch, but hope we've got. You will have to talk to the desired one. For example, does she want to come to expensive restaurants; is she frightened of using the wrong knife; is she worried she can't afford your tastes; is she confused over who pays? Does she want to change the way she speaks? Would you still love her if she drank more expensive plonk? Is she funny, and smart and wise? Strangely, most of the privately educated boys I used to know drank vast amounts of Southern Comfort from their parents' 'liquor cabinets' and developed appalling manners as a result of being horribly spoiled. Some of them were quite nice. Perhaps you are too. It's hard to say, really.

Dear Kaz,
In an effort to 'keep nice' I am writing to you for advice. My problem relates to clothes. Recently I purchased a navy dress, cross-over style, with double gold buttons to the waist. There are no buttons below the waist. Consequently, when walking in windy conditions the skirt tends to blow back, revealing my thighs. While I am not ashamed to expose my thighs on the beach, I wonder if it is acceptable in other

circumstances? Should I sew a hook and eye to restrain the skirt or should I wear suspenders and stockings and not be ashamed to bare my legs?

Canterbury Tall

If you wish to restrain your frock, you will find press-studs in a haberdashery near you. If you wish to display the tops of your lower limbs then you might consider a French maid's uniform or a career in exotic dancing. Strangely, I feel unable to advise you about this.

Dear Kaz,
What do you do if you're playing golf with a friend, helping him to look for a lost ball, when he says, 'I've found it' and you know he hasn't, because you've already found it and have it in your pocket?

Laurie

I have long suspected this sort of behaviour on the part of people who play golf. On the surface, it appears to be a genteel, well-mannered game. I got suspicious when I saw the Prime Minister playing it. I must admit, if I can mix sporting metaphors here, I'm a bit stumped by this one. It depends on many things. If your golf partner is your boss, is larger than you, or is someone to whom you owe money, I'd suggest a polite rejoinder such as: 'Good-oh, sally forth then, old chap'. If you think your friend would enjoy a spot of fisticuffs between greens, then by all means call him a cheat. Perhaps you might wish to consider the possiblity that you have actually found another ball, given up as irrevocably lost by the Prime Minister during his last round with a visiting head of state.

Dear Kaz,
Should a man walk on the street-side of the sidewalk or the house-side?

Justin
North Balwyn

I see. Sidewalks is it now? We have footpaths here, Justin. I can see we are going to have to force a Royal Commission into the minds of North Balwyn. If men take it into their heads to walk on footpaths at any time of the day or night (which is more than women can safely do by the way) they can do it on any side they like, bearing in mind the dangers of poodle poop. And if I get any more letters like this from North Balwyn, I'm going straight to the police.

Dear Kaz,
I enjoy giving a cheery 'Gidday' to fellow pedestrians as I stroll around my neighbourhood. However, I realised recently (I'm a bit slow on the uptake) that it is only 'fellow' pedestrians I make eye contact with— women adopt a grim expression and look into the middle distance. After some thought I realised that this wasn't because they didn't like my haircut, but was a result of a sad but understandable fear of the consequences of talking to strange men on the street. Not wishing to cause discomfort, I adopted the policy of staring at my feet and moving to the opposite edge of the footpath when passing a woman pedestrian. This is a very silly thing to have to do, but the fact is that women can't feel secure walking down the street and that's pretty silly too, to put it mildly. However, I do have the niggling worry that I'm over-reacting, and that a policy of ignoring women is (a) contributing to the problem by accepting that it's reasonable that a woman should feel endangered by a man on the street and (b) rude. What should I do?

Anonymous

Here are a few hints for the man in the street: never jog up behind a woman, especially at night—it can be terrifying; always keep a safe distance between you and a woman—if you wish to pass, cross to the other side of the street; and always keep your hands visible. Much of this is really most important after dark, but it is a reasonable courtesy to save women unnecessary fear from misreading your intentions. During the daytime the problem is not so acute. Unfortunately, most women have been verbally accosted in the street in broad daylight.

A seemingly friendly greeting can suddenly become an obscene comment or unwelcome proposition. It is extraordinary what some men can say to you at 10 am in a crowded shopping centre. This is why many women feel it is safer to ignore a greeting. It takes years of indoctrination and it isn't easy to ignore the 'Don't talk to strange men' rule. By all means continue to be cheery during the daytime, but don't expect effusiveness in return. You don't have to contribute to this dreadful problem by ignoring women in the street, but you must not be offended if they do not respond. If schools would only teach self-defence to young women, much of this problem could be avoided. Perhaps you could help to publicise any self-defence courses run in your area, or encourage the local council to institute some. Thank you for your letter, it's good to know there is some genuine sensitivity out there.

Dear Kaz,
People playing loud music and beach cricket are ruining my summer at the beach. What can I do?

Sandy

Beach etiquette has been eroding for many years. If we are to save whatever we can of it, people must follow some simple rules. It is extremely rude to allow one's beach umbrella to skewer small children during a stiff breeze, also to use somebody's sun-baking position as silly mid-on for beach cricket or to subject 300 metres of sand to Bon Jovi. If your polite requests for peace and quiet are not met, there is little you can do because people who play beach cricket are, as a rule, larger than the rest of us. Go to the Cook Islands, they have beaches and manners there.

Dear Kaz,
My husband sprayed my chrysanthemums with weed killer because he had some left after doing the couch grass and didn't want to 'waste' it. How can I tactfully tell him I don't want such help in the garden, or should I merely be grateful he did not mix the leftovers in my food?

Keen Gardener

You may say quietly, firmly, and with menace, 'Lay off the chryssies, darling, or you'll be sorry'. Inform him of the dangers in having poisons lurching about the environment, and ring your local council to find out where to safely dispose of poisons and other distressing leftovers.

Dear Kaz,
A short while ago an unparalleled event took place in the general area of my abode; someone graffitied a fence in large, vibrant blue letters. Amounts of mud from house renovations had covered the footpath for about four months when the graffiti incident occurred. A citizen had crept out in the night and written 'CLEAN THE MUDDY FOOTPATH' in two-foot letters on the fence and 'MESS' twice with

arrows in the direction of the mud. I am told that one cannot condone this, although one may sympathise with the anguish of the spirit, which was understandably provoked. Is this correct? I am inclined to look upon this graffiti with more tolerance. I thought it humorous by comparison with noble soul graffiti and much better than a scribble. I would be interested to learn your opinon.

Outcast

P.S. The footpath has been cleaned.

I like graffiti. I especially like 'Ian your toast is burning' in Fitzroy and the legendary 'What would you do if God came to Hawthorn tomorrow?' annotated with 'Move Peter Hudson to half-forward' (I am paraphrasing that one from memory). I would rather see a mural or something funny than a brick wall, but it must be difficult for the dwellers behind the wall if they disagree with the sentiments. I don't hold with seat-slashing in trains, but I don't understand why public transport officials don't let people paint all the trams and trains with art or commentary. Instead they are prosecuting artistic 'vandals' and getting rid of the conductors. Life gets more confusing every day. I predict getting 678.4 letters disagreeing with this position.

Dear Kaz,
The peculiar humour of your column has given me many moments of pleasure. Lately, your gift for invention has declined, but perhaps this is inevitable. As one of your moronic graffitists has recently daubed the walls of the school opposite our house, I find your support of him more than usually distressing. I am afraid that you have lost me, you irresponsible, silly woman.

Anonymous

Hold your horses. Is the graffiti a full scale replica of the 'The Last Supper'? Is it funny? Was it a boring blank wall before that which now brightens up the neighbourhood? Or does it just say something racist, sexist, or dull? There's a difference, you know. If you keep writing such self-righteous, rude letters that exclude the facts of the matter I shall consider giving your address to the next writer!

Dear Kaz,
If 678.4 letter-writers disagree with you about graffiti, here's one who

111

agrees. Any teacher knows that the best way to get positive results is not by punishment but through respect and cooperation. We have plenty of empty spaces in our cities which, adorned with colorful murals and witty graffiti, could brighten up our daily lives. I believe this sort of thing is being done in enlightened Scandinavian countries. I'm sure there must be ways and means of encouraging ambitious graffitists to beautify our surroundings creatively and imaginatively, and surely there are artists who would be willing to lead the way. Obviously this would involve planning and patience but such a scheme must deserve encouragement. Wouldn't it be great if this could be a project that a sponsor like BHP would be proud to be connected with?

Wall Flower

Personally, I reckon you can't have too many murals. Wait until the federal election comes along with giant photographs of politicians stuck up everywhere. Imagine coming home feeling a little woozy in the wee hours and finding Paul Keating on the fence.

WE WERE WRONG:

In last week's column the word 'muriel' was replaced by 'mural'. We apologise for any inconveniences.

Clean and Tidy writes of 'twaddle' and 'bleeding-heart apologists for teenage graffiti vandals'. The letter rants about 'so called art . . . almost invariably nothing more than the mindless repetition of signature "tags" over every accessible surface'. Ooh-ah. Just a couple of points.

That's what some people say about million-dollar paintings. It may be true. But much of the rage in teenage graffiti is not necessarily anger, but a fashion for artistic expression. It is not 'mindless'. Many kids have carefully compiled immaculate scrapbooks of their plans, execution and finished works. I do not care for mindless graffiti either, but neither do I care for a society that forces, and by default allows, the time of its young people to become a deep void that can be easily alleviated by writing an expression of love on a dunny wall at 2.30 am. I simply say that there are better things to look at than a blank wall. Or a cigarette advertising billboard. Or a giant, exposed bum used to advertise undergarments. Call me crazy.

11. SEX YOU-ALL HARASSMENT

Whistles; grunts; unsolicited invitations; provocative fiddle-faddle; the great retort collection.

Sexual harassment, like the tax department, takes many forms. It is illegal and defined as unwelcome attention. It can range from a workmate who stares at one's breasts while one outlines the September sales audit process, to unsolicited invitations to give your body whole-heartedly to strangers in the street who leer convincingly, and threats that you'll lose your job if you don't give the boss a hand with his trousers in the back room.

Not all men are like this. Some men treat women as equal human beings, fellow tradespeople, artisans or professionals. They say, 'hello' in the street, instead of, 'Cworrr, I'd like to be up the middle of that!'. These men see a woman as a colleague, a friend, a pedestrian—not a conquest or mindless object. We like these men a lot.

Others, however, upset us, make us angry, make us frightened, patronised, vulnerable, insulted. Generally, we wish they did not exist, and we would be very happy if they were kidnapped and spirited away by aliens, although we would feel a bit sorry for the aliens.

Here are some things you can do about sexual harassment at work: tell the harasser his attentions are unwelcome (some fellers have gained the absurd impression, from soft drink commercials and jingles written by blokes, that women simply adore being ogled and shrieked at in the street), and if the trouble continues, contact your union, a sympathetic supervisor, or the equal opportunities office or Human Rights Commission in your state or territory, if you have one.

That leaves us with the problem of harassment outside the workplace—in dance clubs, bars, the street, the train station, near construction sites, in shopping centres, at home, at parties, at school, and on the beach. A reader calling herself 'Deformed Femininity' wrote to say that she hated such unwelcome intrusions, and felt that there was something wrong with her. 'Keep Yourself

Nice' immediately responded with a coupon for readers to mail in, with space to suggest some witty or crushing responses to a range of harassment techniques. Deformed Femininity had struck a chord. More than 60 coupons and 30 letters were received. They were collated into a special chart which we reproduce here in list form. Letters from two men saying that women should feel complimented by being shouted and leered at in the street were ignored, and it took some restraint on the part of the column not to publish their addresses.

I must caution those of you poised to deliver your crushing comments that sometimes harassers turn nasty. By all means deliver a verbal upper-cut to the ego if there is an acceptable degree of safety—but err on the safe side. It's a jingle out there.

Dear Kaz,
With the summer months coming on, I was hoping you could help me with a very un-nice problem. The Beach Lech. I live in a bayside suburb and, like many others, I enjoy going to the beach to relax, usually by myself. So why is it that I, and most other single women, have to put up with uninvited and unwanted approaches from strange men? Do they feel they have the right to intrude on my solitude simply because I am alone? When hiding behind sunscreen and a hat, should I also erect a large sign: 'Leave Me Alone'? Please advise before I do something downright rude to one of these fellows.

Besieged

Unfortunately for you and the rest of the beach belles, rock videos, advertising of soft drinks and the like have informed a generation or two of boys that girls on the beach are fair game. Got a swimsuit on? Any minute now you'll be expected to pour flavoured milk down your cleavage, hop into the nearest late-model convertible vehicle driven by a vapid chap, or fling yourself onto the next keyboard player with appalling sideburns to come within your field of vision. Whistled at? Now you're supposed to smile sensuously, sidle up to a car full of hoons and offer them your savings account and your body. See what we're up against? We must re-educate the lads that you are reading a book, not aspiring to be a centrefold. Some of them find it very difficult to understand the difference. Also, there are some men who assume that you cannot possibly be happy without the company of somebody with a willy. Whereas we know that the only thing that would really make us fulfilled is world peace and all the shoes we want. Nobody has the right to interrupt you on the beach, unless they have just been rendered legless by a white pointer and are politely requesting your assistance with the other end of a tourniquet. Tell the boys to go away. But don't blame me if you fail to look up at the crucial moment and accidentally give Dennis Quaid the brush-off.

Dear Kaz,
My mother, being a very attractive woman, and also the best fist-fighter on her block as a child, has always been subject to such abuse from men. To any whistle, she responds with a high-pitched whistle and an 'Up yours, Charlie!'. Charlie is a favourite name to use when abusing others. To any lurid suggestions in the way of 'How about it, love?' she may respond, 'Not likely', or 'You've only bought dinner, not the rest of me', or 'I can't dance, I have a wooden leg'. To grunts, etc, the traditional response is, 'What's your problem?' followed by 'Up yours, mate'. To other suggestions she has been known to respond 'On your bike', or to laugh wildly, even hysterically and she does recommend that if the situation gets very uncomfortable you simply start yelling very loudly, 'Fire! Fire!'.

Charlie's Daughter

Dear Kaz,
The whistles and primaeval noises of sexually and socially inept males have always been with us. Try 'the big ignore'. All they want is a reaction, any reaction. To be ignored is very deflating to the male ego. Pinchers and gropers are more difficult to deal with. 'Calling their bluff' can be effective if you have the guts for it, but is definitely not recommended for females under the age of 45! A certain bus driver made elderly passengers cringe with his loud 'compliments'. 'Hello-o-o-o, you gorgeous girl! Where have you been all my life?', he bellowed to one 60-year-old woman. 'Looking for you, you great,

sexy hunk! How about giving us a kiss!', she hollered right back at him. His red-faced collapse was a delight to see.

Granny

What follows is part of a letter from a student at a Melbourne tertiary institution which was plagued by construction site hassling:

Dear Kaz,
At first we subjected the foreman to a barrage of complaints. He assured us that he would speak to the men. I'm sure he did his best but the suggestions continued and became more and more crude. Eventually a copy of the campus policy on sexual harassment was produced, copies were made and displayed everywhere. Many were ripped down or had abuse scrawled on them. We continued and wrote letters and articles for the student newspaper. We made sure the terms sexual harassment and illegal were strongly linked. It worked. A polite approach can be useful, warning: 'Are you aware that what you are doing is sexual harassment? Sexual harassment is illegal. If it continues I will complain to your boss/the police.'

Direct Action

Dear Kaz,
I have been using these and similar responses with a success rate of 90 to 95 per cent for about half-a-century (honestly!). They depend on the fact that the kind of man who uses these and similar approaches knows perfectly well that women HATE them, and he expects an angry, or at least negative, response. At a whistle, turn instantly with a big smile and drop a deep, graceful court curtsey, the full Margot Fonteyn obeisance with delicate hand movement. This usually provokes shocked silence, occasionally it gets a round of applause. Back in the '50s, I trounced a young engineering company estimator who had dedicated his life to embarrassing and humiliating the junior female staff. At a time when four-letter words weren't often heard, he used them constantly and monotonously, and he was a great fiddler with feminine zippers, threatening to rip them open. In fact, a real pain, but of course, never within sight or hearing of management. The lad didn't normally bother me, I was 30-ish and personal assistant to the big boss, but one day we were in a remote office and he decided to have a go at me. I asked him once to stop and then ignored him,

but he kept on and on, and finally after some provocative fiddle-faddle, he reached behind me and undid about a foot of my zipper. Right, mate, I said to myself, and unzipped it myself the rest of the way, peeled off the dress and stepped out of it. HE WAS APPALLED! He jumped back, hissing, 'Christ! What are you doing?', I struck while the iron was hot, 'What the fuck do you think I'm doing, you stupid cunt?', He turned scarlet, and RAN out of the office. It was an instant and permanent cure—he never bothered anyone again. It's fun being old, you have twice as many memories as other people. Remind me to tell you some day about the time I threatened a St Kilda gutter crawler with a fencing foil.

Wynne

Dear Kaz,
Your column this week reminded me of the lady whom I most admire, in her response to a flasher on the train one early afternoon last year. The rest of the passengers knew nothing until this lady spoke with a very clear, well-modulated voice, but almost with a theatrical pitch, and proceeded to tell him what he could do with his equipment that he had out for an airing. Her choice of words was superb and without hysteria I am very sure she taught him a lesson that he will be a jolly long time forgetting. With wonderful aplomb she rose, walked to the train door at her station and announced to the rest of the dumbstruck passengers to keep a sharp eye on him in case he wished to try and impress a more impressionable young teenager. Every eye in that carriage didn't move from him and not surprisingly he left the train shortly thereafter. Wherever you are my dear woman, you are my heroine.

Colleen

Dear Kaz,
A good friend of mine gave this particularly suitable response to a pack of hormonal youths. I thought it worth repeating. Invitation: 'Come here and sit on my face!', Response: 'Why? Is your nose bigger than your dick?'. I hope this is printable.

Scott

Dear Kaz,
My problem is this—I do not enjoy being whistled at. I feel no thrill

from dark, exploratory gazes and thorough visual assessments. Ogling
eyes and glistening, wet lips do not excite me a bit and I am not at
all aroused by suggestive gestures. 'Sweetheart', 'babe', 'honey' (to name
the mildest of unsolicited endearments) are wasted words to my cold
heart and when it comes to physical 'caressment' I cannot even summon
a speck of gratitude from my icy being. I try so hard to feel flattered
by the abundance of compliments, this voluntary offering of esteem,
this utmost of nice etiquette. But it is useless. Kaz, I fear that I am
a failure as a woman. I cannot fulfil this simplest role of a woman.
I know I am an intolerable creature to society. Please advise me.

Deformed Femininity

My dear woman, there are thousands and thousands and thousands of
us unmoved by such pathetic attentions in the street, and the women
who like it are paid to do so by advertising agencies with the account
of a wine and sugary fruit juice drinks company. You are not alone, it's
just that we are all usually alone when it happens. Only the other day
a man in a car leaned from his window and said lewdly, 'Cwoooooorrrr!'.
The only sparkling repartee that sprang to mind at the moment was,
'Oh go away!', to which he replied, 'What's the matter with you? It's
a compliment!'. I'm sorry, but 'Cwoooooorrrr' is not a compliment. 'Gosh,
you're looking healthy', 'I love the way you use verbs', and 'Muted mustard
is absolutely your colour' are compliments. What we need is a ready-
made set of snappy comebacks to insults and sexual invitations on the
street. Would interested readers please fill in the coupon on the right
and send it to 'Keep Yourself Nice'. Copy the coupon and give it to
friends and workmates. Then we can pool our resources and cool our
Romeos.

Readers' suggested responses to:
A WHISTLE

- **Whistle back.**
- A nice, fat raspberry.
- **Unleash trained bull terrier.**
- 'Do you want me to bark or wee on your leg?'
- **'Strewth!'**
- 'Get a puncture kit, dork!'
- **Whistle 'Sisters Are Doin' It for Themselves'**
- 'Some people can whistle tunes.'
- **'Are you working too?'**
- 'Lose something apart from your brain?'
- **Ignore or whistle regimental tune.**
- 'Don't tell me—is it a white-throated cuckoo-shrike?'
- **Just keep walking. (They'll feel stupid.)**
- 'Should I bark, or piss on your leg?'
- **'Act like a tree while I wee on you.'**
- Uncouth finger gesture.

- 'Pardon? I don't speak canary.'
- 'Do I get a free kick?'
- **Take tuba from left pocket and sound long blast upon same.**
- 'Your dog went that way.'
- **A deep, graceful curtsey— the full Margot Fonteyn.**
- 'You have a big future as an electric kettle.'
- **'Lost your dog?'**
- 'Up yours, Charlie.'
- **'Don't whistle—just throw money.'**
- 'I might urinate on your leg.'
- **I thought Harpo Marx was dead.'**
- 'Ha!'
- **Cry. Say husband dead, and five kids to support. Ask for fifty dollars.**
- 'Grow up.'
- **'I hope your dick drops off.'**
- 'And Jesus loves you, too.'

Readers' suggested responses to:
'HOW ABOUT IT, BLONDIE/BABE/GIRLIE?!'

- **'Does the term Herpes Simplex mean anything to you?'**

- 'Not out, John!'

- **Run at subject wild-eyed, singing a nursery rhyme.**

- 'Stick it in the ground and get gravel rash.'

- **'Sorry, it's $6.50 per half hour and I'm fully booked.'**

- 'I thought the garbage was collected yesterday.'

- **'How about what, dickhead?'**

- 'I can't dance, I have a wooden leg.'

- **'Fine, but I should warn you, my name used to be Trevor.'**

- 'How about what? A trip to Paris? Diamonds?'

- **'Yes, please stuff perished fruit down the front of your trousers.'**

- 'Does your mother know you're out?'

- **'Ha! Ha!'**

- 'What's that up your nose?'

- **Ignore it.**

- 'I stopped playing marbles years ago.'

- **'Leave my dog alone!'**

- Feign religious experience.

- **'No thanks, I just had lunch.'**

- 'Go and play pocket billiards.'

- **'Is there somewhere you could be alone?'**

- Do something gross: spit, burp, poke out tongue.

- **'Don't act like a boy.'**

- 'You couldn't afford me.'

- **'Any time you want to kill yourself is fine by me.'**

- 'Your intellect far outweighs mine—it would never work'

- **'No, thanks. I prefer men.'**

- 'How about what, buster!?'

- **'I'd rather kiss a viper!'**

- 'Fancy! I'm on my way to a self-defence class!'

- **'I'd rather be gay.'**

- 'I hope your dick drops off.'

- **'And Jesus loves you, too.'**

121

Readers' suggested responses to:
'WAYYHEY, CWOOR' AND OTHER GRUNTS

- **'I'm a nurse. Please describe the pain.'**
- 'I'll get you some medicine.'
- **Pretend to be an orang-outang.**
- 'What makes you think animal noises turn women on?'
- **'I think you have Blenkinsop's Disease.'**
- 'No need to grunt, I can see you are a pig.'
- **'Your vocabulary is stunning!'**
- 'What's your problem?' or 'Up yours, mate!'
- **'You look familiar—I was at the zoo last week.'**
- 'Now I know a man descended from the apes.'
- **'Is this a reflection of your troubled childhood?'**
- 'Here's 30 cents—call me when you're speaking full sentences.'
- **'Ha! Ha! Ha!'**
- Toss him a packet of ant-acid tablets.
- **Look straight ahead.**
- 'An orang-outang is loose!'
- **Dry retch.**
- Wave amputation scissors.
- **'Try prunes.'**
- 'Blaaaah!'
- **'Have you seen a vet about that?'**
- Snort, meow, woof, blow raspberry, etc.
- **'Still learning baby talk?'**
- 'That's indecent.'
- **'Gee, that's clever!'**
- 'Does the RSPCA know you're out?'
- **'Sorry—I don't speak your language.'**
- Shake head, keep walking.
- **'The pig-pens are at Newmarket.'**
- 'Something's caught in your throat! Shall I thump you!?'
- **'Could you spell that?'**
- 'I hope your dick drops off.'
- **'And Jesus loves you, too.'**

Readers' suggested responses to:
UNSOLICITED SEXUAL INNUENDO

- **A swift karate chop. Laugh like a madwoman!**

- 'Family pet on strike?'

- **Present business card for massage parlor.**

- 'I'm always going to have a headache.'

- **'Put it away, meathead!'**

- 'You're out without your collar again!'

- **'I'd rather kiss a cat's bum.'**

- 'You might be cheap but I'm not.'

- **'You're too small.'**

- Laugh and point at his/her crotch.

- **'Fabulous! I need to try my new rotating cattle-prod!'**

- 'Go somewhere else and pay.'

- **Feign total deafness.**

- 'Not tonight Josephine; or ever.'

- **'How're the wife and kids?'**

- 'Je suspect vous avez un tres petit bon-bon, Wayne.'

- **'Put it in writing and fax yourself.'**

- Use pair of scissors, snip vigorously.

- **'You're not the answer to this maiden's prayer.'**

- Hysterical laughter or begin disrobing on the spot.

- **'Can I have that in writing? I'm a lawyer.'**

- 'Stick it in a bowl of hot custard.'

- **'On your bike!' Hysterical laughter. 'Fire! Fire!'**

- 'I'd have more fun with the employment ads.'

- **'You're so ugly you make my cat bark.'**

- 'Ha! Ha! Ha! Ha!'

- **Inflate a condom. Let off to zoom round importunate solicitor.**

- Talk to a friend in sign language.

- **'I hope your dick drops off.'**

- 'And Jesus loves you, too.'

FRIGHTFULLY HANDY BLANK PAGE FOR YOUR
OWN BLINDINGLY WITTY RESPONSES:

12. AND THE REST

Stan's letter; on the nose; drugs; trams and other vehicular conveyances; getting bounced; the concept of niceness; assorted insults.

This is the fag end of the book, with all the stuff that wouldn't fit anywhere else. But don't let that put you off.

Dear Kaz,
I bet you grew up in a suburb just like North Balwyn. I'll bet you went to a posh private school and I'll bet you have never known a day's deprivation in your life. Ain't it so, that only the securely middle class are entitled to sling off at the middle class? As for me, I grew up poor in the driest, flattest, ugliest little town you ever saw, so I'm quietly greatful now to be living in lovely, leafy, hilly North Bawls. However, I'm not a member of Neighbourhood Watch or Rotary, I support Community Aid Abroad and Amnesty International (with money). I'm agnostic, and I've voted for the Democrats ever since Labor turned so right-wing. Can all these things redeem me, or must I move to North Carlton in order to become ideologically sound? Please advise.

> Generalisations Are Odious
> North Balwyn

I really, really wish people would stop writing letters from North Balwyn—it is so ineffably depressing. If it's not asking how to serve escargots and which side of the footpath to walk on, it's chock-a-block with words like 'middle class', a phrase never before mentioned in this column. Live wherever you can, but don't come whingeing to me about growing up in Tennant Creek.

Dear Kaz,
Your recent column infers that you are a devotee of the JJJ radio station. Determinded to keep myself 'alternatively nice' I tuned in and was rewarded by the sound of what I believed to be an unsocialised person sc...sc...scratching what passes for music on this station. A teenage nephew informs me that this style of popular music has

126

something to do with hip-hop fashion and is popular in LA with rapper gangs. Further investigation led me to view, or be assaulted by, video clips of such maestros. Their philosophy seems quite Tory, and based on materialism, and it seems compulsory for females to appear barefoot and bikini-ed and pose and pout with exaggerated immature sexual provocation. Is it appropriate for an etiquette columnist to declare her avid consumption of a station that promotes such cultural dr... dr... drivel? Emily Post would not approve and would probably suggest you switch your dial permanently to the beautiful music station.

My G...G...Generation

Oh dear. Let's start at the beginning. You infer incorrectly. I did not imply that I was a slavish listener to the radio station. The snippet I referred to in an earlier column was heard on the way to Perth airport after my brother's wedding. The station in question does not always play rap and hip-hop. You won't find an argument with me about the nature of most rock video clips. If it's not models flouncing about with vacant expressions on white horses, it's pre-pubescents as sex objects. But if that's drivel, what's beautiful music? The '70s hits of Barry Manilow? Fleetwood Mac's offerings? At least JJJ tries on occasion to support local talent and keep the music industry moving forward. Wasn't Emily Post Wilbur's wife in 'Mr Ed'? If I listened to conventional wisdom about what was appropriate, I suppose I would be wearing a vapid expression and cavorting with a white horse. It may interest you to know that some rap music clans in the United States have banded together to release anti-drug and anti-violence songs and Salt and Pepa, a female rap duo, also have a good line in non-sexist lyrics, which is more than Nancy Reagan ever did.

Dear Kaz,
I have been given two fragrances for Christmas. Which would be more suitable for a tea dance—Purple Prurience or Total Inertia?

Quandary

Please remember that politeness to others dictates the sparing use of fragrances. Have you ever BEEN in a David Jones lift? As most fragrances are made from substances such as muskrat testicles, Agent Orange and monosodium glutamate, a well-bred woman will ask any dancing partner for a list of his allergies.

127

Dear Kaz,
My friends at school keep offering me drugs, and I'm too scared to take any. I've read that you never know what's in them. It's mostly dope and speed. They give me a hard time. How do I say no without being a jerk?

Chris

You never know what is in drugs you buy at school, especially, I seem to remember, the cream buns. If you don't want to lose face, I suggest you effect a very cool expression and say, 'I've had enough of the stuff to last me a lifetime. I'm just not interested any more', and look mysterious. I wouldn't worry too much about looking like a jerk, even if you decide to say, 'Nah, I don't want any', because there's nothing terribly attractive about possible side-effects including vomiting, criminal courts, the mind of a North American game show hostess and overdosing. If they still think you're a jerk listen to Lou Reed albums. That'll fix 'em.

Dear Kaz,
A former friend has behaved so dreadfully that I never want to see him again. How do I tell him?

Horrified

Over the telephone.

Dear Kaz,
I am at desperation point and fear I may soon act in a manner not consistent with the laws that protect the community at large. Why are the majority of tram travellers so unthinking and selfish? They refuse to heed pleadings to move down the back of the tram, thereby forcing the driver to leave frustrated, and often wet, would-be passengers on tram steps while there is still room at the back. Others who are grossly overweight and/or accompanied by large bags, stand in the doorways, thus obstructing those who wish to finish their journey. My reaction has advanced from tut-tutting to mild abuse and lately, standing on toes. Can you suggest some remedies that will satisfy my desire to punish these half-wits?

Toe Treader

By rights the tram driver should not move off until everybody has been herded into the nooks and crannies. Conductors with experience in sheep-herding are always invaluable. If you wish to make people get out of your way without being rude (an admirable ambition), you may wish to try the More Personal Space Loony method. If you behave very strangely, singing 'Goodnight Irene' at the top of your voice, undulating your eyebrows expansively while whistling, I think you will find commuters giving you a fairly wide berth and helping you off the tram at your designated stop.

Readers who don't live in Victoria can substitue 'bus' or 'train' for 'tram' whenever they feel the urge.

Dear Kaz,
A man got on the almost-empty tram. He asked me spitefully if I had paid a fare for the shopping bag next to me. The next day, I got on a crowded tram where one man was occupying two seats with his legs wide apart and a bag on the third. He let me stand. Should I have sat on his knee, kicked him near the junction or got off and rung the police?

Indignant

It is perfectly appalling the way people disport themselves on trams these days. You were right to put your shopping bag next to you or the spiteful traveller might have sat next to you and engaged you in unseemly conversation. However, on a crowded tram, the etiquette is quite clear. All elderly, frail, obviously pregnant, or tired workers should have a seat whenever possible, regardless of gender except in the case of pregnancy. You are permitted to say to a sprawler, 'Excuse me, could I trouble you to make some space?' or, 'Would you mind moving that bag, china, my plates are killing me'. Check for war veterans before you sit down. Should you encounter a churlish response you may call a connie and he or she will sort the matter out quick smart. If not, judicious use of the indispensable hat pin may be employed.

Dear Kaz,
My friend and I went into town with the empties to leave at the bottle department to be recycled. There was discovered a whole, corked bottle of 18-year-old red wine from the Barossa Valley! We tentatively approached the flexi-teller to see if the cheque had been cleared. We

had money in the bank! We bought 'The Age'. On the way home, we stopped off at our best friends' house—most valued and trusting friends. We ransacked their house in their absence in the vain hope of finding their stash of marijuana. Lo and behold, we found the stash and made off with a bit of it. Now we are suffering from acute guilt pangs. Should we confess all? Buy them lavish presents? Or fabricate a story of burglary?

Shame-Faced

Frankly, I am completely appalled. Appalled. I will go so far as to say flabbergasted and almost hornswoggled. With friends like you, who needs bank charges? The funny thing about being so dishonest is that you will eventually mistrust the very people you have swindled. You will begin to think everyone may well be as untrustworthy as yourself. You must realise that if drugs are going to turn you into some kind of social thug, it's time to hit the lime cordial. You must confess and throw yourself on the mercy of your friends. You deserve whatever you get, and while I hope for a gracious pardon, you must prepare yourself for the possiblility of shock and a demand for mowing the lawn weekly until the turn of the century. Now behave yourself.

Dear Kaz,
I am nice. I'm quite sure almost everyone who has ever met me would say so. My problem is that I'm not sure I want to stay nice. There are major drawbacks in being nice. If you want to succeed professionally you have to be 'ambitious', 'dynamic' and 'results-oriented'. Have you ever seen a job advertisement that has the word 'nice' in it? I haven't got a job. If you want to succeed with females and you are absolutely, overwhelmingly nice you run the risk of being labelled a wimp, or even more unfair, a homosexual. I own one pair of yellow socks and I like flowers and poetry. I haven't got a girlfriend. I am sick of being nice. How can I become an aggressive, competitive, results-oriented individual?

(Editor's note: more followed about the dangers of giving your Bankcard to prostitutes and an ambition to busk in Bourke Street on an airmail edition of the 'Financial Times' but it has been edited out.)

Penniless And Lonely Heterosexual

Frankly, I don't see why you can't be nice and ambitious at the same time. Unfortunately, I have absolutely no idea what 'results-oriented' means. Perhaps, if you really want a girlfriend, you could strike a balance between describing women as 'females' and being 'over-whelmingly' nice. I cannot advise you on how to become a selfish dork. Gay men may be considered generally as nice, but they are also gainfully employed in all levels of society. Perhaps you'd better front up to the CES again.

The following letter was scrawled, and guesses have been hazarded when it proved indecipherable:

Dear Kaz,
How can I KEEP nice when I'm not nice now? I have never been nice since I was a little girl brought in to be introduced to callers who were NICE people and kissed me wetly through their veils. So I soon became NOT NICE. A little girl who wouldn't change into a clean dress when visitors came, or brush her hair or wash her filthy face and hands and her bare legs with dried blood on them from the delicious scratching of mozzie bites. I've always found the NICE people are NOT NICE, in fact many of them are really nasty. So please, I want to keep myself nasty, anyway—are you NICE? It must be hard, with a face like yours, with a shamrock mouth and holding a clawhammer and three-pronged fork, doing obviously something NOT NICE but perhaps trying to be useful, which isn't NICE. It's nicer to be nasty and wear no sticky muck on the face and cut those Medusa-like locks and wear wool in winter and swim in real rushing water up past Omeo and climb a MOUNTAIN and get all sweaty and red in the face and sing poetry that RHYMES and climb the fire-tower and yell loudly all over the blue place.

Nasty

Phew! It seems an unfortunate formative experience at a young age has led you to adopt a narrow and sometimes misguided definition of 'nice'. Personally, I don't think lipstick in itself is a necessarily corrupting influence, but let me recommend the upper reaches of the Mitta Mitta River near the junction of the Snowy Creek for swimming. Last time I climbed a fire-tower near Omeo I saw three tiger snakes, so keep yelling loudly across the blue place to scare them off. That is not a picture of me, it is a cartoon used for what newspaper people call a 'dinkus'. The plural is dinki.

Dear Kaz,

I try really hard to keep myself nice. I have two lovely children in private schools and live in a really nice suburb. I drive a Volvo and wear those outrageously expensive but really comfortable Reeboks. I even have a really adorable cocker spaniel named Sebastian. My problem is this: I am really left-wing at heart and eschew all of these things, but none of my friends believe me! What should I do?

Madeleine
North Balwyn

AND:

Dear Kaz,

I am a socialist, feminist, anarchist and have lived in North Balwyn for four years. It's a terrible strain, but it's an excellent place for chewing holes in the fabric of traditional society. I can't move, as the cat, dog and children can't bear to be uprooted because of their traumatic formative years and child-minder respectively. What are your suggestions for survival in such a place?

Caz, (with a 'C')
North Balwyn

Eschew? Chewing? North Bawls gets more bizarre every day. Life can get lonely when you're forced to rationalise your life by yourself over a short black. (What an anarchist does with a child-minder is beyond me.) Why don't you two get together. You can both sound dreadfully concerned over a flagon of red wine—the Drug of Choice for arm-chair socialists.

Dear Kaz,

On behalf of my husband and myself, please advise, as we are most desirous of improving our situation. We aspire to a residence in North Balwyn. But my husband won't buy one unless I go back to my second job as a topless bar person, in his hotel. Hardly suitable. What second job should he get?

Mandy Fortesque ESQ

Only the other day somebody accused me of inventing the letters to this column. As if I had to. No, I'm still getting this sort of thing. Women

132

signing themselves esquire, and perspiring to North Balwyn. It is a real worry. Get on with you.

Dear Kaz,
I don't see why you have the right to tell people what to do. Everyone should have the right to do anything they like, dress the way they want to and say whatever they please.
Vive La Difference

Quite. This philosophy is very charming in theory, but liable to lead to World War III or the total destruction of the ozone layer in practice. I recognise the trivial nature of some of this column. I do not suggest that the return of flared trousers as a fashion item is more serious than life in Beirut for a single mother. But etiquette is all about caring about other people and diplomacy. Or at least it should be. Should people be able to blow cigar smoke in your face in a crowded train carriage? Beat their wives? Annex Papua New Guinea on Thursday? Test nuclear bombs on the Launceston golf course? Personally, I'd advise against it. I have no qualifications to advise others except that people write and ask me to consider their little quandaries. Besides, I'm not rich enough to do whatever I want to. That's why I'm not living in the Cook Islands with a dead ringer for the young Cary Grant. And if I could say whatever I liked, I'd probably be the Sultan of Brunei.

Dear Miss Cook (sic),
I love chess with a passion. I adore its nuances and infinite variety. Each game is like an adventure and I can never wait to find out how it ends. Truly, I don't mind losing, the game's the thing. Recently I have taken to playing regular games with an ignorant bore who not only does not appreciate the game fully, but has no respect for the niceties and etiquette. To him it is a mind game where ego is all. His fear and loathing of losing is such that he goes to the very border of acceptable behaviour to win. For instance, at that time of every game, usually called the 'middle game', he will defer making his move. He will get up and make coffee, ask to use the telephone, make inane chatter until I am totally frazzled. If he makes a bad move he will ask to have it again (sometimes three or four times a go). Should he be losing, he will beat his breast, tear at his hair and complain that his brain hurts. If winning, he will gloat aloud with running comments

on how his troops will methodically and mercilessly destroy my own in a great and glorious victory thereby proving that his is the superior brain. He has even taken to sticking a clarinet up his left nostril and playing 'When the Saints Go Marching In' (rather badly, I might add) to further unnerve me. My question is this. Is it etiquette to kill this slob?

Exasperated

Without in any way accepting the bit about the clarinet, here is my advice. I went to three different state (now primary) schools. Wherever I was, I found that 'I'm not going to play with you any more' or 'I don't want to play with you' fairly brilliantly transmitted the general feeling, per se, that I didn't want to play with them anymore, and that I wouldn't. No, you can't kill him. That would be cheating.

Dear Kaz,
May I make a plea for a modern rule of etiquette when using an automatic banking machine? I suggest that all people in the queue should stand to the side, about a metre away from the user of the machine. One can feel very threatened by a big male person standing behind one (I am a female). I try to use the facility only in daylight and when the shopping centre is busy, but the snag is then the length of the queue.

Concerned

Well, I see what you mean. It is absolutely true that many large male persons may be collectively described as the salt of the earth. Several of my acquaintance would rather tie themselves in a knot before threatening a person of either sex. A nervous banker, however, is unlikely to tell them apart from homicidal maniacs just by looking. So, lads, how about giving women a bit more room to move in the queue? Women must keep their end of the bargain by not allowing anybody to butt into the queue ahead of the male with manners. This can be achieved by saying rather loudly, 'I'm sorry, you shall have to go to the end of the queue. This sensitive prince among men is no doubt about to make a timely withdrawal. I suggest you do the same or I shall render the machine unusable by chaining myself to it with three half hitches!' or something that takes your fancy at the time.

134

INDEX

missionary position   83, 95
Mormons   40, 46
Morris Elite, 1957   33
mud wrestling   4
Nana   4, 20
napkins   60, 62
National Party   6, 34, 51, 84, 104
no children allowed   85
Nobel Peace Prize   3
nuclear engineer   9
pink flannelette nighties   17, 70
Pinochet, Augusto (General)   64
preferential voting system, the   61
Reagan, Nancy   127
Reed, Lou   128
RINSO   82
Rotarian baiter   86
Russell, Bertrand   96
serviettes: see napkins
single mother   11, 12, 48

skiffle board   39
squid   60, 68
steamer trunk   10
stocking in the petrol tank   107
suits, safari   17
swamp gum stump   42
tampons   78
tea-bags   65
telephone etiquette   5, 6, 56
tertiary syphilis   13
thighs   20, 107
tiara   17, 25, 50
tofu   32
topiary   47
Trade Practices Commission   3
Tupperware/exotic marital aids
   48
Tweed Heads caravan park   28
vikings, shickered   52
woggle   48